A
DICTIONARY
OF
AMERICAN
HOMOPHONES
AND
HOMOGRAPHS

HAROLD C. WHITFORD

A
DICTIONARY
OF
AMERICAN
HOMOPHONES
AND
HOMOGRAPHS

*with illustrative examples
and exercises*

TEACHERS COLLEGE PRESS, TEACHERS COLLEGE,
COLUMBIA UNIVERSITY, NEW YORK, 1966

To the Memory
of Two Colleagues Distinguished as
Teachers of English to Foreigners

ROBERT J. DIXSON

THOMAS LEE CROWELL, JR.

Preface

This dictionary is primarily designed to help foreign students of English who have even greater difficulty with "confusables" in our language than do a number of native American high-school and college students. Part I, the major section, lists over 1,000 homophones—pairs of words identically pronounced but different in spelling and meaning. Part II deals with 160 homographs—pairs of words identical in spelling but differing in pronunciation and meaning. For each homophone and homograph there are included single or multiple definitions, pronunciation equivalents, and one or more illustrative sentences. Part III consists of an additional list of 800 less frequently used homophones; and a substantial number of oral and written exercises in Part IV make this volume usable as a textbook as well as a reference book.

H.C.W.

Contents

A
DICTIONARY
OF
AMERICAN
HOMOPHONES
AND
HOMOGRAPHS

Part I

A DICTIONARY OF HOMOPHONES

(Pairs of words that have the same pronunciation but with
different spellings and different meanings)

A

A (rhymes with day) the first letter of
the alphabet:—The letter a precedes
the letter B.

—eh an exclamation of surprise:—Eh!
Did you say you had just gotten married?

Abel (rhymes with cable) son of Adam
and Eve and murdered brother of
Cain:—Cain killed Abel.

—able having ability or power:—Chief
Justice Holmes was a very able jurist.

accept (rhymes with Dick crept) take
or receive willing from another person:—She will accept him if he pro-
poses marriage.

—except but:—We found all our next-
door neighbors at home except John,
who was away at camp.

acts (rhymes with facts) deeds:—Every
adult is responsible for his acts.

—*axe (rhymes with tax) a long-
handled bladed cutting tool used for
felling or cutting down trees:—That
woodsman is very skillful with his
axe.

ad (rhymes with bad) advertisement:—
Mary answered a classified ad for a
typist and got the job.

—add put with something else, increase:—If you add 3 to 6, you get 9.

addition (rhymes with a mission)
something added to or put with
something else:—They are building
a new addition to our school.

—edition a one-time printing or press
run of a book, magazine, or newspaper:—I bought an early morning
edition of the "Times."

adds (rhymes with lads) increase:—A
day off from work adds to one's
pleasure.

—adze a large sharp-bladed tool used
to plane rough wood smooth:—The
workman bestrides a log while he
uses an adze.

adieu (rhymes with anew) Goodbye! a
goodbye or farewell:—After the
movie was over, we bade our com-
panions adieu.

—ado trouble, fuss, bustle, delay:—The
Senator's empty speech was much
ado about nothing.

adze see **adds**

affect (rhymes with correct) alter,
change:—The President's death
might greatly affect the stock market.

—effect cause, bring about:—The judge
managed to effect a reconciliation
between the estranged couple.

aid (rhymes with paid) assistance,
help:—The Red Cross sent aid to
the flooded city.

—aide a military officer serving as an
assistant to a high-ranking official:—
The general gave the marching
orders to his aide.

ail (rhymes with nail) hurt, bother,
cause suffering:—What ails you;
don't you feel well?

—ale a malt beverage similar to beer:—
I had a bottle of ale with my dinner.

air (rhymes with care) the atmosphere,
the mixture of oxygen and nitrogen
that we breathe:—We opened the
windows so as to let in some fresh
air.

Note: A superimposed asterisk indicates a close if not exact equivalent. A superior
numeral indicates one of a pair of homographs listed on pages 55–62.

1

—ere before:—I must ask you a question ere you leave.

—heir one who will inherit property willed to him:—Robert is his father's sole heir.

aisle (rhymes with dial) a straight path or passage from the rear end to the front row of a theatre, church, etc.:—Look! The bride is coming down the center aisle with her father.

—I'll contraction for I shall or I will:—I'll think over your offer for my car and let you know.

—isle a small island (land surrounded by water):—Ireland is known as the Emerald Isle.

ale see ail

all (rhymes with ball) every bit or unit of a substance or group:—All men must register for the draft.

—awl a sharp-pointed tool for punching holes in leather:—An awl is an important tool of the shoemaker.

all ready (rhymes with call Teddy) ready, prepared, all set:—The buyers of the house were all ready to sign the contract when the owner suddenly died.

—already by now, by this or that time, previously:—Here it isn't yet five o'clock and it is already dark outside. I looked for Tom at the party, but he had already left.

all together associated in a group, assembled:—We children were all together at Christmas.

—altogether completely:—That meal we just had at the hotel was altogether unsatisfactory.

all ways (rhymes with fall days) from every standpoint:—That candidate for mayor is in all ways an excellent choice.

—*always all the time:—He is always late to work.

allowed (rhymes with a crowd) permitted:—Dogs are not allowed inside the hospital.

—aloud audibly, so as to be heard:—Being alone, the old man spoke his thoughts aloud.

allude (rhymes with a food, accrued) refer to something or someone indirectly:—In mentioning "man's best friend," the speaker was alluding to a dog.

—elude escape from:—The fleeing convict was able to elude his pursuers.

allusion (rhymes with collusion) an indirect reference:—"The Bard of Avon" is an allusion to Shakespeare.

—*illusion something that looks different from what it really is:—Magicians seem to work miracles by means of illusions.

aloud see allowed

already see all ready

altar (rhymes with Walter) the table and wall facing the church congregation and behind the officiating priest:—During the mass the priest knelt before the altar.

—alter change, remodel:—Since Nell's dress was too large, she had to have a dressmaker alter it to her size.

altogether see all together

always see all ways

amend (rhymes with offend) change, improve:—The members voted to amend the constitution of their club.

—emend correct errors in a document:—Many editors have tried to emend seeming errors in Shakespeare's texts,

an (rhymes with can) definite article used before words beginning with a, e, i, or o and before unpronounced h:—We say an apple, an orange, an honor; but a hymn, a universe.

—Ann a girl's name. Also spelt Anne.

ant (rhymes with can't) the common crawling six-legged insect—Ants got into our picnic basket and spoiled the food.

—aunt the sister of one's father or mother or the wife of one's uncle:—Mother's three sisters are my aunts.

ante (rhymes with can't he) (slang) to pay up:—When Mr. Jones's son drove into another car and damaged it, Mr. Jones had to ante up for the repairs.

—anti against:—Anti-Christians are opposed to Christ, Christians, and their religion.

—auntie affectionate term for aunt:— I love my Auntie Jo.

any way (rhymes with many say) without restriction as to kind of way or method:—You can do that job any way you want, provided it gets done.

—anyway no matter what happens, despite what occurs or may result:— He applied for a scholarship, but he said that he didn't want to go to college anyway.

arc (rhymes with park) a curve, part of the outline of a circle:—That road makes a large arc around the mountain.

—ark the ship Noah sailed in during the great flood:—Two kinds of each animal were carried in the ark.

are (rhymes with bar) present tense plural of the verb to be:—Are you a student?

—our (unstressed) possessive pronoun of the first person plural:—We took our umbrellas as it looked like rain. See **hour—our**

—R the 18th letter of the alphabet:— Readin', 'Ritin', and 'Rithmetic were known as the three R's.

area (rhymes with carry a) a large space or region, geographical or otherwise:—Behind the school is a large area which is used as a playground.

—aria a song from an opera:—The soprano sang a lovely aria from "Manon."

ark see **arc**

a rye (rhymes with apply) a drink of rye whiskey:—Let me have a rye and water.

—awry amiss, in disorder or confusion:—When the war came, all our plans for travel abroad went awry.

ascent (rhymes with a rent) a climb, a rising:—It's a steep ascent up Mont Blanc.

—assent say yes or agree:—The teacher will assent to her class's request for a picnic.

assay (rhymes with obey) analyze ore to determine the usefulness of a mineral deposit:—The mining company decided to assay samples of ore from a new mine.

—essay try or attempt:—When in Paris we always essay to carry on our conversations in French.

assent see **ascent**

assistance (rhymes with a distance) help, aid:—When the old lady slipped on the sidewalk, two strangers rushed to her assistance.

—assistants plural of **assistant,** a helper or aide:—Our butcher has two assistants.

aster (rhymes with faster) a common flower with many petals around a yellow disk:—A bowl of freshly cut asters brightened up our living room.

—Astor surname of a famous American:—The Hotel Astor is in New York's theatrical district.

ate[1] (rhymes with state) past tense of eat:—We ate a hurried breakfast this morning.

—eight the number that comes next after seven:—I ate eight dates.

attendance (rhymes with ascendance) state or fact of being present:—Our best student has had a perfect attendance this semester.

—attendants plural of **attendant,** persons serving or waiting on a personage of high rank or a bride:—The king entered the palace with his attendants.

auger (rhymes with logger) a screw-like winding tool used for boring holes:— The carpenter used an auger to drill a hole in a plank.

—augur indicate some future happening, foretell good or evil, portend:— The efficient way Jack started out on his job augurs well.

aught (rhymes with bought) anything:— Do you know aught of Nan's whereabouts?

—**ought** auxiliary verb expressing obligation less positively than "must":—I ought to help my wife wash those dishes, but I'm not going to.

augur see auger

aunt see ant

auntie see ante

aural (rhymes with coral) referring to the sense of hearing:—That child's aural sense was impaired by illness.

—**oral** spoken, not written:—The judge accepted both oral and written testimony.

away (rhymes with a day) some distance off, absent:—I was only ten feet away from the accident when it happened. Our neighbors have gone away for the summer.

—**aweigh** raised off the bottom of the sea and placed on board ship, said of anchors:—With anchors aweigh, we set sail for Europe.

awful (rhymes with waffle) unpleasant, painful, dreadful:—Haven't we been having awful weather lately?

—**offal** refuse, animal or other waste material:After cutting up the deer, the hunters threw the offal to the dogs.

awl see all

awry see a rye

axe see acts

aye (rhymes with cry) yes:—"Aye, aye," cried the sailor in response to his captain's orders.

—**eye** the organ one sees with:—I have perfect vision in one eye.

—**I** first person pronoun, ninth letter of the alphabet:—I know that there are two i's in "finish."

B

B (rhymes with tree) the second letter of the alphabet:—I received a B in my math exam.

—**be** infinitive of the common verb to be:—I like to be busy.

—**Bea** a nickname for Beatrice:—I am very fond of Bea Rogers.

—**bee** the honey-making insect:—Yesterday Bob got stung by a bee.

baa (rhymes with spa) the crying or bleating sound made by sheep:—Baa, baa, black sheep, have you any wool?

—**bah!** an interjection of disbelief or contempt equivalent to "Nonsense!"

bad (rhymes with had) not good, evil:—I have a very bad cold which was caused by last week's bad weather. George will become a criminal if he keeps in bad company.

—**bade** past tense of bid, direct, order:—John's mother bade him wipe his muddy feet on the doormat before entering the house.

bah! see baa

bail (rhymes with fail) money handed over to the court as security for the reappearance of an arrested person at trial:—The judge set the accused burglar's bail at $5,000.

—**bale** a large package of compressed raw cotton ready for shipment or storage:—Hundreds of cotton bales stood on the pier ready for shipment abroad.

bald (rhymes with called) hairless:—My grandfather is bald-headed.

—**bawled** past tense of bawl, cry loudly or weep:—The baby bawled all night because he was hungry.

bale see bail

ball (rhymes with fall) a rounded or spherical object used in sports such as baseball, tennis, or golf:—The pitcher threw the ball to second base.

—**bawl** cry or weep loudly:—Hear that noisy drunk bawl for another drink.

balm (rhymes with Mom, Tom) something that soothes or heals:—The discharged workman felt that his wife's sympathy was balm to his injured feelings.

—**bomb** destroy by a severe explosion:—In World War II enemy aircraft would bomb London and Berlin.

band (rhymes with land) 1. a long narrow strip of material, often circular, such as a rubber band, a wrist-watch band:—A simple band of gold served as Dorothy's wedding ring. 2. an organized group of persons particularly a musical ensemble:—We heard the band play marches in the park.

—**banned** past tense of **ban,** abolish, forbid:—A regulation banned smoking in the classrooms.

bands (rhymes with lands) plural of **band:**—The doctor wound bands of surgical dressing around the wound.

—***banns** an engaged couple's announcement before a church congregation of their marriage intentions:—Next week John's and Mary's banns will be published.

—***bans** third person singular of **ban,** forbid:—Our landlord bans all animals from his apartment house.

banned see **band**

banns see **bands**

bans see **bands**

bard (rhymes with hard) a poet:—Shakespeare is often referred to as the Bard of Avon.

—**barred** past tense of **bar,** hinder or prevent:—On account of his low grades, Ralph is barred from playing on the football team.

bare (rhymes with care) uncovered, naked:—In her beach costume her arms and legs are bare.

—**bear** 1. the largest long-haired wild animal:—The Russian bear is a national symbol. 2. carry, endure:—That Mexican woman bears her basket of wash upon her head. Medicine helped the patient to bear his pain.

baron (rhymes with Karen, heron) a nobleman with that title:—Baron Ochs is an amusing character in the opera "Der Rosenkavalier."

—**barren** 1. empty:—The trees are barren of leaves in the winter. 2. childless:—He divorced his barren wife and remarried.

baroness (rhymes with narrowness) a baron's wife.

—**barreness** state of being empty, unproductive:—That large unfurnished room was depressing because of its barreness.

barred see **bard**

barren see **baron**

barreness see **baroness**

base (rhymes with face) 1. low, mean, socially inferior:—In olden days a man of noble birth was not permitted to marry a girl of base birth. 2. a foundation or military installation:—That house rests on a base of concrete. The United States has an air base in Iceland.

—**bass**[1] the lower notes in instrumental or vocal music:—In the orchestra a bass viol plays the lowest or bass notes, Roger sings bass in our choir.

based (rhymes with raced) past tense of **base,** pattern after, found, build on:—That novel is based on a real life story.

—**baste** 1. pour hot juices over roasting meat:—Mother has to baste the turkey many times before it is done. 2. sew temporary seams:—The tailor bastes the woolen suit material together before stitching it on the machine.

bases[1] (rhymes with cases) plural of **base,** a foundation or a major point in baseball:—The fielder caught the fly ball and put out two players on bases.

—**basses** 1. two or more men singing a bass part:—A double male quartet has two basses. 2. two or more bass viols or double basses in an orchestra:—Players of double basses often stand when they play.

bask (rhymes with task) pleasantly warm oneself in the sun or indoors before an open fire:—Let's go to Bermuda this winter and bask in the sun all day.

—**Basque** describing the Basque people of Spain:—The Basque language is unique.

bass[1] see **base**

basses see **bases**[1]

baste see **based**

bawl see **ball**

bawled see **bald**

bazaar (rhymes with the car) an oriental market or a store selling imported items:—I bought my oriental rugs in a bazaar in Damascus.

—**bizarre** strange, exotic, eccentric:—Some of that cubistic painter's works seem very bizarre to the uninitiated.

bb (rhymes with t.b., Phoebe) small round lead shot for an airgun:—I loaded my air-rifle with bb shot.

—**Beebe** a surname.

be see **B**

Bea see **B**

beach (rhymes with teach) the sandy part of the seashore:—While their elders went swimming in the surf, the little tots played on the wet beach.

—**beech** a hardwood tree and the wood from that tree:—Our doors are made from a variety of beech.

bean (rhymes with mean) type of vegetable such as string bean, coffee bean, lima bean:—Boston is famous for its baked beans.

—**been**[1] British pronunciation of the past participle of the verb **to be**:—How have you been, old top? See **been**[2]—**bin**

bear see **bare**

beat (rhymes with street) 1. strike or hit:—We beat the rugs every spring to get out the dust. 2. conquer, win from:—Charles beat me at tennis.

—**beet** a dark red edible vegetable root:—We had Harvard beets for lunch.

beau (rhymes with go) a wooer, a male escort and admirer of a young woman:—Jane is very popular and has a new beau every week.

—**bow**[1] 1. a curve or a curved stick such as a bow and arrow or violin bow:—It is hard for a boy to stretch a man-sized hunter's bow. 2. a knot made in a tie or a ribbon:—Morris wears bow ties.

bee see **B**

Beebe see **bb**

beech see **beach**

been[1] see **bean**

been[2] (rhymes with tin) American pronunciation of the past participle of **to be**:—Have you been to Radio City?

—**bin** a storage room for coal, vegetables, etc., usually in the cellar:—Our coal-bin is nearly empty. See **bean—been**.[1]

beer (rhymes with fear) a malt alcoholic drink, a bottle or a glass of beer:—Let's have a beer before lunch.

—**bier** the stand or pedestal upon which rests an embalmed body before or during a funeral:—Throngs passed by the bier to take a final look at the great man.

beet see **beat**

bell (rhymes with sell) an inverted metal shell with a clapper inside that shaken against its sides causes a ringing sound:—The church bells ring a half hour before the service.

—**belle** a beautiful, much sought-after young lady of the upper social classes:—Gloria was the belle of the ball, and everyone wanted to dance with her.

berry (rhymes with carry) a fruit such as the strawberry or blueberry:—We had raspberry pie for dessert.

—**bury** cover up, hide, entomb:—The loss of his job made him bury his face in his hands. Where did they bury your grandfather?

berth (rhymes with earth) a bed on a ship, train, or plane:—Two can sleep in a lower berth on a Pullman sleeper.

—**birth** act of being born, the arrival of a newborn baby into the world:—December 25th. commemorates the birth of Jesus Christ.

better (rhymes with wetter) 1. comparative of good:—James has a better car than Joan. 2. improve:—Sam can better his condition by getting a raise in salary.

—**bettor** one who bets or wagers money on horse races or other sports events, or on games of chance:—That bookie has to pay off the winning bettors.

bi (rhymes with try) a prefix meaning two:—That newspaper is a bi-weekly publication and comes out every two weeks.

—**buy** bargain, purchase:—The radio says that peaches are a good buy this week. Where did you buy your car?

—**by** preposition showing agency or direction:—That picture was painted by Rubens. Our friend drove by our house without stopping.

—**bye** 1. used in such expressions as goodbye (farewell), by the bye (incidentally):—Bye the bye, have you color television?

bier see **beer**

bight (rhymes with light) a loop in a rope:—The small boat was secured to the dock by a bight.

—**bite** puncture, tear or gnaw flesh, bones, or food with the teeth:—Our neighbor's dog will bite strangers.

billed (rhymes with killed) past tense of **bill,** send to a debtor a bill or statement of amount owed:—The doctor billed me for an x-ray he had taken of my chest.

—**build** construct a house, etc.:—Let's build a garage in back of our house.

bin see **been²**

birth see **berth**

bite see **bight**

bizarre see **bazaar**

blanch (rhymes with chance) whiten or bleach, turn white:—The sight of the accident made her blanch with fear.

—**Blanche** a girl's name.

blessed¹ (rhymes with rest) past tense of **bless,** commend another person or object to God:—During the service the priest blessed the sacramental wine.

—**blest** said of something honored by God or very dear to one:—Our late mother has gone to the Isles of the Blest.

blew (rhymes with few) past tense of **blow,** circulate or force out air under pressure:—The wind blew very hard and ripped off the roof of a nearby house.

—**blue** the color of the sky or sea in fair weather:—The American flag consists of three colors—red, white, and blue.

bloc (rhymes with stock) a small group of people or nations organized to maintain their special interests or privileges:—The farm bloc forced the passage of the agricultural appropriation bill in Congress.

—**block** 1. shut off, prevent:—The Democrats will block the passage of that tax bill in the Senate. 2. the smallest section of a city, usually a quadrangle bounded by four streets:—We live on a quiet block.

blond (rhymes with fond) yellow or otherwise light-colored:—Their living-room is furnished with blond furniture.

—**blonde** a girl with light coloring, especially one with light-yellow hair:—It has been said that gentlemen prefer blondes.

blue see **blew**

boar (rhymes with door) a full-grown male pig domesticated or wild:—Boar hunting is a favorite sport in Europe.

—**bore** 1. to drill a hole through wood, etc.:—The electrician had to bore through heavy beams when he wired the old house. 2. tire, cause restlessness, ennui:—Those incessant hillbilly tunes bore me. 3. past tense of **bear,** endure, carry:—That invalid bore his troubles cheerfully.

—**bower¹** (also rhymes with goer) one who makes bows:—Bowers used to make bows, and fletchers used to make arrows.

board (rhymes with ford) 1. a planed length of wood thinner than a plank:—I made a table out of a few boards. 2. meals served to paying guests:—John pays fifteen dollars a week for room and board. 3. get on a vehicle or ship:—We board our plane at noon.

—**bored** past tense of **bore** 1. drill a hole:—I first bored a hole in the board before trying to screw it to the frame of the table I was making. 2. be tired of or jaded with:—After an hour of dull lecturing, we became very bored with our instructor.

boarder (rhymes with hoarder) one who pays for his meals at a boarding house:—The Whites have taken in three boarders this fall.

—**border** an edge or boundary:—On the border between France and Spain lie the Pyrenees.

bode (rhymes with code) portend, indicate:—That patient's bad cough bodes him no good.

—**bowed**[1] 1. past tense of **bow**[1], draw the bow across a stringed instrument:—We thought that that violinist bowed extremely well. 2. bow-shaped, curved:—Her legs are bowed.

bold (rhymes with sold) brave, courageous, aggressive:—By a bold attack the smaller army put the larger enemy forces to flight.

—**bowled** past tense of **bowl**, pitch balls in a bowling alley:—Our team bowled better than our opponents.

bolder (rhymes with colder) comparative of **bold**, brave, courageous:—Henry is bolder than his weaker sister.

—**boulder** or **bowlder** a large rock standing by itself:—There are many boulders on this rocky beach.

bole (rhymes with stole) bark or covering of a tree trunk:—There's moss growing on the bole of that elm.

—**boll** pod of the cotton and flax plants:—Cotton pickers must extract the bolls of cotton from the plants.

—**bowl** 1. a round dish with a deep inside:—We have a wash-bowl in the bathroom. 2. play in a bowling alley:—Last night I bowled 160.

bomb see **balm**
border see **boarder**
bore see **boar**
bored see **board**
born (rhymes with torn) be brought into the world:—Lincoln was born in a log cabin.

—**borne** 1. past participle of **bear** 1. carry:—The football champion was borne on the shoulders of the admiring spectators. 2. endure:—His pain was more than could be borne.

borough (rhymes with furrow) a political sub-division, often of a city:—New York City's City Hall is in the Borough of Manhattan.

—**burro** a small donkey used to carry a rider or transport baggage or kept and ridden as a pet:—We rode burros down the steep sides of the canyon.

—**burrow** dig underneath the ground and hide there:—The moles burrow underneath our lawn and make ridges.

bough (rhymes with now) the arm, limb, or branch of a tree:—Peter climbed up into a bough of our old maple.

—**bow**[2] incline the head as a mark of respect:—While we were having our dinner in a restaurant, we saw a fellow diner bow to us.

bouillon (rhymes with cool Don) a light, clear soup made from meat stock:—We like jellied bouillon in summer.

—*****bullion** (rhymes with full sun) gold and silver money or heavy bricks or bars made from these metals:—Bullion is usually stored in the vaults of large banks.

boulder see **bolder**
bow[1] see **beau**
bow[2] see **bough**
bowed[1] see **bode**
bower[1] see **boar**
bowl see **bole**
bowled see **bold**
boy (rhymes with toy) a young lad:—The Browns have a boy and a girl.

—buoy a floating marker in a river or harbor indicating a channel or obstruction:—The buoys in this harbor are painted red.

braid (rhymes with fade) 1. a band made of twisted or woven strands of hair or threads:—Marcia likes to wear her hair in braids. 2. an ornamental edging or decoration sewn on uniforms or on a woman's dress:—That admiral is covered with gold braid.

—brayed past tense of bray, the sound a donkey makes:—The hungry donkey brayed loudly.

braise (rhymes with days) cook meat slowly in a little water:—We had braised veal for lunch.

—brays plural of bray, a donkey's voice:—That sick donkey's brays are driving us mad.

—braze join or weld two pieces of metal together by heating and using an alloy:—The mechanic had to braze the two broken pieces of brakedrum together.

brake (rhymes with take) that part of a car's mechanism that slows down or stops a car:—I have good brakes on my car and can stop quickly. I seldom use my hand-brake.

—break smash or knock to pieces:—If you drop a glass on a hard stone, the glass will break.

brayed see braid

brays see braise

braze see braise

breach (rhymes with teach) 1. break an opening or passage through a wall, etc.:—The soldiers made a breach in the outer walls and stormed the castle. 2. a violation of a custom, law or trust:—It is a breach of good manners to eat peas with a knife.

—breech the tube in a gun where the ammunition is placed:—I opened the breech of my shotgun and put in a cartridge.

bread (rhymes with head) the common baked food made of wheat or other grain:—I have to buy a loaf of bread for dinner.

—bred past tense of breed, bring forth, cause, or train:—Those vanished slums bred crime. That young man is very well-bred.

break see brake

bred see bread

breech see breach

brewed (rhymes with rude) past tense of brew, prepare tea, coffee, etc.:—Mary brewed us a cup of tea before we left.

—brood 1. a group of young birds such as chickens or a family group of children:—The Browns have a brood of six children. 2. feel sorry for oneself:—Even though you did lose the race, don't brood over it all the rest of your life.

brews (rhymes with screws, whose) plural of brew, a hot drink such as tea or coffee:—Tea and coffee are popular brews.

—bruise a yellow or dark-colored mark left on the skin from a knock or blow:—I got a nasty bruise on my leg from a fall on the ice.

bridal (rhymes with tidal) having to do with a bride or a wedding:—When Ellen was married, she wore her mother's bridal dress.

—bridle the headpiece and reins connected with the horse's bit that are used to curb or control the animal:—I put on the horse's bridle, harnessed him to the wagon, and drove off.

broach (rhymes with coach) begin or suggest a subject for discussion:—I want my employer to be in a good mood when I broach the matter of a raise in pay for myself.

—brooch a decorative breastpin usually jeweled:—I gave my wife a diamond brooch for her birthday.

brood see brewed

brows (rhymes with cows) eyebrows, the hairline above each eye:—When I asked Edith a personal question, she raised her brows in surprise.

—browse briefly examine book after book in a library or bookstore:—I like to browse in old bookstores when I am in New York.

bruise see brews

bruit scatter or spread news:—Newspapers like to bruit about the latest doings of society people.

—brute an animal or a man like an animal, a clumsy and often cruel person:—A horse is a dumb brute. That drunk is a brute to his wife and frequently beats her.

build see billed

bullion see bouillon

buoy see boy

burro see borough

burrow see borough

bury see berry

bus (rhymes with muss, fuss) a large motor vehicle that transports the general public:—I take a bus to work every morning.

—buss kiss:—Her husband leaned over and gave her a buss.

bussed (rhymes with dust) kissed:—Before going to work Mr. Smith bussed each of his daughters.

—bust 1. the chest of a woman:—My mother has a large bust. 2. also the head and shoulders of a person reproduced (sculptured) in marble, bronze, etc.:—Rodin carved busts of many famous people.

but (rhymes with cut) 1. conjunction similar in meaning to however:—Mary can sing, but she can't play the piano. 2. a preposition meaning except:—I like every vegetable but carrots.

—butt run headfirst against, charge at:—That angry cow began to butt her head against the fence.

buy see bi

by see bi

bye see bi

C

C (rhymes with me) 1. the third letter in the alphabet:—There are two c's in "soccer." 2. (Cap.) Roman numeral meaning 100.

—sea the ocean:—Four sailors were lost at sea during the storm.

—see 1. look at:—Let's see a movie tonight. 2. visualize, perceive:—I can see better with my glasses than without them.

C's (rhymes with bees) plural of C:—There are two c's in "accept."

—seas plural of sea, ocean:—Those whalers have sailed the seven seas.

—seize grasp, hold on to:—I saw the dog seize the meat with his teeth.

cache (rhymes with dash) secrete:—During the war France and Germany had to cache their art treasures in caves.

—cash money:—Near the end of the month I became rather short of cash.

caddie (rhymes with daddy) a boy employed to carry a golfer's bag of clubs:—One caddie will serve for four golfers if they are playing together.

—caddy a small can or box for holding tea:—Our tea caddy is empty.

Cain (rhymes with gain) son of Adam and Eve and slayer of his brother Abel:—Cain's sin was fratricide.

—cane 1. the thick jointed stalk of the sugar cane or bamboo:—The native laborers cut the sugar cane and then it is shipped to the sugar mills. 2. a walking stick:—Grandfather always carries a cane.

calendar (rhymes with gallon, sir) a chart or charts issued annually showing the relation of the numerical days of the months to the name days:—Every business office has a calendar.

—calender process paper so as to make it shinier and smoother: We chose a calendered paper on which to print our illustrations.

cane see Cain

cannon (rhymes with tannin) the largest of guns, a piece of heavy artillery:—That army's defense line is backed by long-range cannon.

—canon a rule or law:—John's discourtesy to his hostess violated the canons good taste.

cant (rhymes with grant) special language of a certain class of people, jargon:—The slang dictionaries give many examples of thieves' cant.

—can't contraction of cannot:—He can't swim, can he?

canvas (rhymes with plan us) a heavy cloth used for tents and sails:—During the squall, the sailors shortened the canvas and rode out the storm.

—canvass visit a number of people in order to get their aid, opinions, or support, or to sell them merchandise:—We shall canvass the neighborhood seeking votes for our candidate for mayor.

capital (rhymes with map it all) 1. the administrative city of a state government:—Albany is the capital of New York State. 2. money or invested funds:—With very small capital he started a factory.

—capitol a large public building where the national or state legislatures meet:—Domes surmount the roofs of most state capitols.

carat (rhymes with garret) a measure for expressing the relative fineness of gold:—My wife wears an eighteen-carat gold breastpin.

—caret a mark made between two printed, typed, or written letters to indicate an omission:—Having misspelled the word "stood" by leaving ut the second "o," I inserted a caret between the "o" and the "d" and wrote the missing "o" at the top.

—carrot the familiar orange-hued vegetable root:—We had diced carrots and peas with our steak.

cash see cache

cask (rhymes with ask) a large barrel used for holding liquids:—On board ship they kept a cask of whisky.

—casque a steel helmet or head-piece, part of a suit of armor:—The knight fastened on his casque and rode off.

cast (rhymes with fast) 1. throw:—The little boy cast a stone into the water. 2. the plaster copy of an original sculpture:—We had a large cast of the Venus di Milo in our classroom.

—caste social rank in human society:—In India the Brahmins are of the highest caste.

cause (rhymes with laws) the reason for:—The cause of the fire that burned down the church was undetermined.

—caws plural of caw, the sound made by a crow:—The air was filled with the caws of the ravenous crows flying over the cornfield.

cede (rhymes with need) grant, hand over, transfer:—The Indians were persuaded to cede Manhattan Island to the Dutch.

—seed small grains from a plant that replanted in the earth grow upwards into grass, flowers, vegetables, etc.:—We like to look at the colored pictures of flowers in the seed catalogs.

ceiling (rhymes with wheeling) the top or roof of a room:—That old house has a very high ceiling.

—sealing the act of moistening and closing the flap of an envelope:—The stamping and sealing of the envelopes for the form-letters took all afternoon.

cell (rhymes with bell) 1. a prison, usually a small room with a barred window:—The prisoner stared at the outside world from his single cell. 2. a single unit such as a dry-battery cell.

—sell transfer ownership in property for payment or consideration:—My jeweler tried to sell me an expensive wrist-watch.

cellar (rhymes with teller) the basement of a building:—He keeps his wine in a cool cellar.

—seller who who sells merchandise, a merchant or other dealer:—The seller used to say: "Let the buyer beware."

cense (rhymes with tense) perfume with incense as in a church:—The priest will cense the place around the altar.

—***cents** plural of **cent**, a penny:—That newspaper costs five cents.

—***scents** plural of **scent**, an odor or perfume:—That department store's cosmetic counters are redolent with scents. Mother scents her handkerchief with lavender.

—**sense** 1. feel:—One could sense his impatience at being kept waiting in line for tickets. 2. good reasoning ability, practical thinking:—John showed good sense in preferring going to college to loafing. 3. one of the five senses:—His sense of taste is keener than his sense of smell.

censer (rhymes with denser) a metal container of burning incense used in religious services:—The priest carried a censer and swung it.

—**censor** an official who forbids publication or sale of a book or the showing of all or part of a play or movie:—In certain states many movies are cut by the censors before they can be shown.

cent (rhymes with bent) a penny:—My newspaper didn't cost a cent. Someone gave it to me.

—**scent** a perfume or other distinctive smell:—Our flower garden was full of violets with their delightful scent.

—**sent** past tense of **send** 1. transmit:—I sent a letter to Mother last night. 2. dispatch a person:—I sent Sam on an errand to the drugstore.

cents see **cense**

cereal (rhymes with material) grain such as wheat, oats, etc. and the breakfast food made from it:—Cornflakes are my favorite cereal.

—**serial** a story on the radio or in a magazine or newspaper that is continued from issue to issue or from day to day:—I read that popular novel first as a serial in a ladies' magazine.

Ceres (rhymes with wearies) Roman goddess of agriculture:—At harvest time the Romans worshipped Ceres.

—**series** a number of related events:—A series of small thefts was traced to a housemaid.

champagne (rhymes with campaign) a prized effervescent French wine:—Champagne was served at the wedding reception.

—**champaign** a flat open field often cultivated with grass or flowers:—That large estate has a large champaign of daisies.

chance (rhymes with dance) 1. opportunity:—His chance for promotion is good. 2. risk:—Don't take a chance and drive through a red traffic light.

—***chants** (rhymes with pants) plural of **chant**, a song sung in church to a ritual mass:—That choir sings chants as responses.

chanty (rhymes with can't he, panty) a song sung by sailors in time to their work:—While hauling in a net full of fish, the sailors sang a chanty.

—**shanty** a small dilapidated building crudely constructed:—Those hoboes live in a shanty on the edge of a river.

chary (rhymes with merry) 1. careful:—Susan is very chary of her collection of dolls. 2. stingy:—Ralph is very chary of his car and won't lend it to anyone.

—**cherry** the red fruit of the cherry tree:—Mother baked us a cherry pie for dessert.

chased (rhymes with haste) 1. engraved:—My grandfather's watch was chased with the design of an eagle. 2. the past tense of **chase**, run after, pursue:—The policeman chased the thief for two blocks before capturing him.

—**chaste** pure, virginal:—Susannah was too chaste to submit to her tormenters.

cheap (rhymes with sleep) 1. not expensive:—Potatoes are relatively cheap. 2. inferior, of poor quality:—She was wearing a cheap, unbecoming dress.

—**cheep** monotonous call or cry made by small birds—The sick sparrow gave a few cheeps and died.

check (rhymes with neck) 1. a bank check:—I pay all my bills by check. 2. hinder, stop:—When her husband started to swear, she would check him.

—**Czech** a native of Czechoslovakia:—Dvořak was a Czech composer.

cheep see **cheap**

cherry see **chary**

chews (rhymes with whose) third person present form of **chew**, bite into food before swallowing, masticate:—Tom chews his food well before swallowing.

—**choose** select:—I shall choose a matching tie to go with this suit.

chic (rhymes with seek, the ch has the sound of sh) stylish:—Last Easter Sunday Marie wore a very chic hat.

—**sheik** an Arab chieftain:—Many sheiks live in the desert.

Chile (rhymes with Billy, hilly) a large country in southwest South America:—Copper is exported from Chile.

—**chili** red pepper used in cooking:—That pizza pie is full of hot chili.

—**chilly** quite cool or cold, said of the weather:—It's chilly enough for a topcoat this morning.

choir (rhymes with wire) a group of singers, especially at a church service:—Martha sang in her church choir for fifty cents a Sunday.

—**quire** a total of 24 identical sheets of paper:—I bought a quire of writing paper.

choler (rhymes with dollar) anger, indignation:—When Tom saw the big boy beating the little boy, his choler rose.

—**collar** linen or other material worn around the neck:—I need a new shirt; my collar and cuffs are frayed.

choose see **chews**

choral (rhymes with moral) pertaining to a choir or other band of singers:—We heard both instrumental and choral music at the concert.

—**coral** the pink, red, and white stonelike substance from a tropical ocean reef:—Janet has a necklace made of pink coral.

chord (rhymes with Lord) three or more musical notes played simultaneously:—The accompanist struck a chord on the piano, and the choir started to sing.

—**cord** a piece of sturdy string or twine:—I tied up my packages with stout cord.

—**cored** past tense of **core**, cut out or remove the center or inedible part of an apple:—Mother cored the apples before baking them.

chute (rhymes with boot) a slanting runway used for sliding goods from an upper to a lower level:—We have a laundry chute in our house.

—**shoot** discharge or fire off a gun usually at some object:—Don't shoot deer out of season; it's against the law.

cider (rhymes with wider) a drink made from the juice of freshly pressed apples:—We drink lots of sweet cider in the fall.

—**sider** one who sides with, supports, or champions another:—The Democratic nominee was cheered by his siders.

cite (rhymes with light) mention or list:—Teachers often cite examples of heroism to their pupils.

—**sight** view, appearance, eyesight:—The sight of land cheered the homesick passengers on the steamer. He has good sight and will be accepted by the Army.

—**site** place, location:—Where is the site of the new city hall to be?

clack (rhymes with black) the sudden sharp noise of wood or metal struck against wood or other material:—

The wind caused the venetian blinds to clack against the windowpane.

—claque members of the audience paid by an opera singer or actor to applaud him loudly during the performance of an opera or play:—Caruso's claque generally stood in the balcony.

clammer (rhymes with hammer) one who digs for clams:—At low tide there were many clammers digging for clams in the wet sand.

—clamor a noisy outcry of a group that is usually demanding something:—Each year at city hall a number of citizens regularly clamor for a tax reduction.

claque see clack

clause (rhymes with laws) a group of related words having a subject and a verb:—A complete sentence is called an independent clause.

—claws the nails on the paw of an animal such as a dog, bear, cat, etc.:—That cat has sharp claws.

climb (rhymes with time) ascend, go up:—That invalid can't climb trees.

—clime geographical region, place, or section:—In the winter-time the northern rich seek the warmer southern climes.

close² (rhymes with goes) shut, lock up:—Be sure and close the windows if it rains.

—clothes wearing apparel:—Each spring my wife thinks she needs new clothes.

coal (rhymes with stole) hard black carbon mined and burned in a furnace to provide heating or power:—We have three tons of coal in our cellar.

—cole a cabbage-like leafy vegetable.

coaled (rhymes with fold) past tense of coal, fill or load with coal:—After the ship was coaled, she left port.

—cold 1. opposite of hot, low in temperature:—The winter weather in the North is cold. 2. a head cold, coryza:—I can't seem to lose my cold

which I have had now for three weeks.

coarse (rhymes with force) opposite of fine or refined:—A coarse screen has larger holes than a fine screen has.

—course 1. way, direction:—The navigator took a NNW course. 2. a college academic subject:—At Cornell I took a course in English Literature.

coax (rhymes with jokes, soaks) urge or plead with one to act, and often succeed in persuading one to do something:—I heard John's wife coax him to buy her a fur coat, but he refused.

—cokes plural of coke, a popular soft drink:—After my long hot walk, I drank two cokes.

cocky (rhymes with rocky) arrogant, show-offish, aggressive:—James has been very cocky ever since he won the tennis match.

—khaki the brown cloth used in soldiers' uniforms, also the color itself:—The sergeant wore a khaki shirt.

coco (rhymes with loco, spoke o) the palm tree on which coconuts grow.

—cocoa powdered cacao seeds with the fat removed, similar to chocolate, also a hot drink made from the powder:—I like a cup of cocoa for breakfast.

coffer (rhymes with offer) a metal box designed to hold money or jewels:—That miser has lots of gold in his coffers.

—cougher one who coughs or clears his throat:—That cougher is disturbing the whole theatre audience.

cokes see coax

cold see coaled

cole see coal

collar see choler

colonel (rhymes with eternal) an Army officer in rank above a major:—Theodore Roosevelt was a colonel.

—kernel the inside heart of a nut or the seed of wheat, corn, etc.:—In canning corn, machines strip the kernels from the corn-cob.

complement complete, offset, or balance:—James's wife's rashness is complemented by his prudence.

—**compliment** praise another, say something nice about him:—I want to compliment my hostess on the fine cake she has baked.

comptroller (rhymes with consoler) the chief finance officer of a corporation in charge of controlling expenditures:—Smith was appointed comptroller of the Southern Railroad.

—**controller** a person or object that controls or regulates:—The electric locomotive is put in motion by advancing the controller.

coo (rhymes with who, stew) the soft sound made by a dove, or a baby's sounds of pleasure:—The music made the baby coo.

—**coup** a bold stroke or act resulting in a significant victory:—Napoleon executed a bold coup at Austerlitz.

coolie (rhymes with truly) a Chinese common laborer often exploited:—Coolie labor built the Chinese wall.

—**coolly** in a cool, unexcited manner:—When Tom's doctor told him his condition was serious, the patient took it coolly.

coop (rhymes with soup) a small low shed for housing chickens:—We used to have a chicken coop in the backyard.

—**coupe** a two-door automobile with a hard top:—She drives a 1956 Ford coupe.

coral see **choral**

cord see **chord**

core (rhymes with door) the central part of anything—an apple, a magnet, etc.:—I don't eat apple cores.

—**corps** an organized group of soldiers or working civilians:—Last Sunday members of the First Army Corps played baseball in the park.

cored see **chord**

corps see **core**

cougher see **coffer**

council an advisory or governing board:—That city is run by the City Council.

—**counsel** advice:—Tom's father gave him very good counsel about getting a job.

coup see **coo**

coupe see **coop**

course see **coarse**

cousin (rhymes with dozen) son or daughter of one's aunt or uncle:—My father's brother's son is my first cousin.

—**cozen** cheat, defraud:—Henry tried to cozen his sister by urging her to buy his worthless watch for twenty-five dollars.

coward (rhymes with Howard) one who is shamefully afraid:—James was too great a coward to admit to his mother that he had accidentally broken her glasses.

—**cowered** past tense of **cower**, shrink away in fear:—The disobedient boy cowered before his angry father.

cozen see **cousin**

crape (rhymes with tape) a thin, black, crinkled cloth used especially for mourning garments:—At the funeral the deceased's widow wore a black crape veil.

—**crepe** a woven silk cloth of various colors:—Mary was wearing a light-blue crepe dinner dress.

creak (rhymes with seek) the squeaking noise made by a closing door or a loose floorboard:—The floors of an old house often creak when you walk on them.

—**creek** a small river or a small inlet from the sea:—We went fishing in the creek just outside of town.

crepe see **crape**

crews (rhymes with shoes) plural of crew, a group of seamen, etc.:—The crews of the various ships met on land for a game of baseball.

—**cruise** 1. a leisurely trip by air or sea with stops at various ports:—Last winter we took a cruise to the West Indies. 2. said of an urban taxicab that is being driven empty while the driver is looking for a passenger:—Too many taxis cruise in midtown Manhattan and congest the traffic.

cue (rhymes with blue) a hint, sign, or keyword:—During a play each actor listens for his cue so that he will know when his speaking part comes.

—**Q** the 17th letter of the alphabet:—Mind your P's and Q's.

—**queue** a line of people before a ticket window:—There was a long queue standing in front of the opera house, waiting to purchase tickets.

currant a small red or black edible berry:—I am very fond of red-currant jelly.

—**current** 1. a flow of electricity, air, or water:—It was hard to row our boat against the heavy current. 2. recent, existing now:—Have you read his current novel?

cymbal (rhymes with thimble) one of a pair of round metal disks struck together to make a crashing or ringing sound:—A symphony orchestra always needs a musician to play the cymbals.

—**symbol** the representation of something else:—The eagle is the symbol of America, the cross a symbol of Christianity.

Czech see **check**

D

dam (rhymes with Sam) a horizontal obstruction of earth or concrete used to hold back running water so as to form a pond or lake:—The Hoover Dam is one of the world's largest.

—**damn** an exclamation of annoyance or anger:—Damn that train, is it late again this week?

days (rhymes with gaze) plural of day:—Many old people have seen happier days.

—**daze** confuse, enchant, transfix:—The large number of Christmas gifts tended to daze the children.

dear (rhymes with fear) 1. an adjective expressing love or affection:—This ring belonged to my dear mother. 2. expensive:—Strawberries are too dear to buy in winter.

—**deer** swift four-legged forest animals with horns or antlers:—The two hunters shot and killed a deer apiece.

dense (rhymes with tens) thick or with its many parts close together:—The pioneers had to hack their way through a dense forest.

—***dents** (rhymes with tents) plural of dent, a depression in a piece of metal:—I ran my car into the side of a truck and have two dents in my right fender as a result.

descent (rhymes with is bent) 1. a going downwards:—The path made a steep descent. 2. parentage, ancestry:—He is of Irish descent.

—**dissent** expressed disagreement:—There was more assent than dissent to the proposal to cut taxes.

desert² (rhymes with avert, accent on the second syllable) abandon, leave:—The Browns will desert New York and move to Los Angeles.

—**dessert** a sweet dish usually served at the end of a meal:—We had a steak dinner with ice-cream for dessert.

dew (rhymes with you) the moisture on the grass in early summer sunny mornings:—The children got their feet wet from the dew on the lawn.

—**do¹** perform, act:—I do what I please when on vacation.

—**due** adjective referring to the time when payment is expected:—All of that store's charge customers must pay their bills when due or within thirty days after making a purchase.

die (rhymes with try) 1. cease to live, be, or exist:—Without air a person will die. After midnight the noise of the merrymakers in the next apartment began to die down.

—**dye** color or tint, said of cloth, hair, etc.:—Marta used to dye her hair a light blue.

dissent see **descent**

do¹ see **dew**

do² (rhymes with go) the first tone of the musical scale, followed by re, mi, fa, sol, la, te, do.

—**doe** a female deer:—We saw a buck and two does in the woods.

—**dough** the result of combining flour and liquids into a mixture that is then baked into bread, cake, etc.:—The cook poured the dough into a cake-tin and put it into the oven.

doc (rhymes with lock) short for **doctor**:—How long will I have to stay in bed, Doc?

—**dock** a projecting narrow landing place for a boat, a pier or wharf:—The stevedore unloaded our baggage onto the dock.

doe see **do²** and **does²**

does² (rhymes with goes) plural of **doe**, a female deer.

—**doze** sleep lightly after a meal, take a nap:—After a heavy meal Arthur fell into a light doze.

done (rhymes with gun) past participle of **do**, perform:—That student has done a very good term paper.

—**dun** 1. dull brown in color:—Farmer Jones has a dun cow. 2. press for payment of a debt:—All the local stores are dunning Blake for the merchandise he bought months ago and which is still unpaid for.

dough see **do²**

doze see **does²**

draft (rhymes with laughed, staffed) 1. in the U.S. Selective Service system the drawing of a young man's name for compulsory military service:—John Jones was inducted into the Army during the first year of the draft. 2. a bill of exchange used for payment.

—**draught** a current of air:—Please close that window; I don't like to sit in a draught.

dual (rhymes with fuel) double, two:—

That instruction automobile has dual controls, one for the teacher and one for the learner.

—**duel** a contest or fight between two opponents:—The two enemies fought a duel with swords and one man was badly wounded. We watched the duel of words between the two Senators.

ducked (rhymes with trucked) past tense of **duck**, dodge or avoid:—Angered, Jim swung his fists at Tom, but Tom ducked and wasn't hit.

—**duct** a closed metal passage for air, used in heating, air-conditioning, etc.:—A large duct for circulating hot air passes directly over my desk.

due see **dew**

duel see **dual**

dun see **done**

dye see **die**

E

E's (rhymes with fees) plural of **E**, the fifth letter of the alphabet:—There are two e's in "feet."

—**ease** comfort:—The rich man lives a life of ease.

earn (rhymes with burn) be paid money for one's services:—That worker earns fifty dollars a week.

—**urn** a large bell-mouthed vase for holding ashes or flowers:—The deceased's body was cremated and his ashes placed in an urn.

earnest (rhymes with sternest) true, sincere:—It is my earnest wish that you succeed in your chosen profession.

—**Ernest** a male given name.

ease see **E's**

eaves (rhymes with leaves) plural of **eave**, the projecting joint between the roof and the top of a house:—Their attic was packed to the eaves with junk.

—**Eve's** possessive form of **Eve** a girl's name:—Adam was Eve's husband.

edition see addition
effect see affect
eh see A
eight see ate
elude see allude
emend see amend
emit (rhymes with befit) give out rays, odors, etc.:—We saw the stove emit black smoke.
—*omit (rhymes with the hit) leave out or neglect:—Don't omit to say good-bye to your hostess.
ensure (rhymes with endure) make certain, guarantee:—In order to ensure the prisoner's return to court, the judge made him put up bail.
—insure cover or protect the insured against loss, destruction, or death:—We want to insure our house against fire. He has his life insured for $20,000.
entrance¹ a door, gate, or other opening to a building, park, etc., opposite of exit:—There is a revolving door at the entrance to that restaurant.
—entrants those entering contests, competitions, etc.:—There are five entrants signed up for the mile race.
ere see air
Ernest see earnest
essay see assay
Ethel (rhymes with bethel, methyl) a girl's name.
—ethyl a kind of alcohol:—Ethyl alcohol is safer to drink than poisonous wood alcohol.
Eve's see eaves
ewe (rhymes with true) a female sheep:—Those ewes are feeding their lambs.
—U 1. the 21st. letter of the alphabet:—There are three u's in "unusual." 2. also U-shaped:—Drivers cannot make a U-turn at that intersection.
—yew a kind of evergreen tree:—There is a yew planted near that house.
—you second-person pronoun:—I'll lend you my car if you like.

ewer (rhymes with tour) a large pitcher used to hold water for washing:—She poured water into the bowl from a copper ewer.
—your possessive form of you:—Here is your book.
—you're contraction of you are:—You're attending Columbia, aren't you?
except see accept
eye see aye
eyelet (rhymes with pilot) a small hole for a shoestring to pass through:—My sport shoes have brass eyelets.
—islet a small island:—The Thousand Islands consist of many small islets.

F

fain (rhymes with train) like to, gladly do:—Your guest would fain drink to your health.
—fane religious shrine or church:—The Tudor Protestants desecrated the Catholic fanes.
—feign pretend:—Some lazy employees feign illness in order to avoid going to work.
faint (rhymes with paint) 1. lose consciousness:—We saw the criminal faint when he heard the judge's harsh sentence.
—feint pretend to strike another person so as to throw him off his guard, a term used in boxing:—The spectators saw the boxer feint with his right and drive his left into his adversary's stomach.
fair (rhymes with care) 1. just, equitable:—Was it fair for George to quarrel with his children, bequeath his money to strangers and leave his children unprovided for? 2. a fiesta, exhibition:—We saw interesting agricultural exhibits at the country fair. 3. light-colored:—Their child is a fair-haired boy. 4. clear weather:—Tomorrow will be fair and warm. 5. mediocre:—That student's marks are just fair.
—fare 1. get along, manage:—How does she fare with her new job? 2. cost

of transportation:—Our local bus fare is fifteen cents.

fairy (rhymes with Harry) a tiny supernatural being:—Cinderella's fairy godmother won a husband for her. Titania was the Queen of Fairies.

—**ferry** a ship for transporting people and cars across a river or lake:—There are still a few ferries that cross the Hudson River.

false (rhymes with Paul's) not true, pretended, imitation:—She wears false teeth, hair, and eyelashes.

—***faults** (rhymes with salts) plural of **fault**, an error, mistake, or bad habit:—One of Marcia's faults is her ill temper.

fane see **fain**

fare see **fair**

fate (rhymes with late) one's lot or his fortune or misfortune:—To be drowned was the poor child's fate.

—**fete** a party or celebration:—Our church held a lawn fete in July.

faults see **false**

faun (rhymes with lawn, dawn) a mythological deity half man half goat:—Fauns and nymphs are usually pictured near streams or wooded places.

—**fawn** 1. a young deer:—We saw a doe and her two fawns. 2. seek favor from a superior by flattery and subservience:—Bill always fawns on the boss.

faze (rhymes with stays) intimidate or deter another person from doing something:—The fact that his opponent was larger and heavier than he did not faze the experienced boxer.

—**phase** a certain time period of a life or an operation:—The next phase of the General's life was a tempestuous one.

feat (rhymes with seat) an unusual achievement, a remarkable act:—The plunge of a daredevil in a barrel off Niagara Falls was a great feat.

—**feet** plural of **foot**:—Most of us have two feet.

feign see **fain**

feint see **faint**

ferry see **fairy**

fete see **fate**

few (rhymes with sue) a small number or quantity:—Few people know where that author lives.

—**phew** an exclamation of reaction against pressure or unpleasantness of any other kind:—Phew! but that was a close call. (Said of an accident that the speaker has barely avoided)

file (rhymes with mile) 1. a grooved flat tool for wearing down metals, shaping fingernails, etc.:—I carry a nailfile in my purse. 2. a drawer or cabinet of drawers for storing letters, etc.:—We have several steel files in our office. 3. a single line:—A long double file of trucks was waiting for the red light to change to green.

—**phial** a small bottle containing medicine, perfume, etc.:—She keeps a phial of French perfume on her dressing table.

—**phile** suffix meaning lover of:—A bibliophile is a lover and collector of books.

fill (rhymes with Bill) pour or load something into a container so that it is full:—At breakfast I fill a small glass with orange juice and drink it.

—**Phil** short for Philip, a boy's name.

fillip (rhymes with still up) zest, interest:—A dash of mint added a fillip to the roast lamb.

—**Philip** a boy's name

filter (rhymes with kilter, quilter) a screen or other substance that removes impurities present in a liquid or smoke:—He smokes cigarettes equipped with filters.

—**philtre** a love potion believed to inspire the drinker with love for the person offering the drink.

fin (rhymes with tin) waving projecting membrane of a fish used to steer it through the water:—In cleaning a fish, remove the fins as they are not edible.

—**Finn** a native of Finland.

find (rhymes with blind) 1. locate, track down something:—I cannot find my missing necklace. 2. think, consider:—I find TV very boring.

—**fined** past tense of **fine**, levy or exact money for an infraction of the law:—The judge fined the drunken motorist fifty dollars.

finish (rhymes with diminish) end or complete:—We will finish our spring semester in May.

—**Finnish** pertaining to Finland or the Finns:—The Morgans have a Finnish cook.

Finn see **fin**

Finnish see **finish**

fir (rhymes with her) a common evergreen tree or the boards made from that tree:—There was a shady grove of firs around the lake. Our doors are made of fir.

—**fur** the hair of an animal such as the bear, fox, mink, etc. often left on the hide and made into coats, neckpieces, etc. or used as trimming:—Mary has a new fur coat.

fisher (rhymes with wish her) one engaged in catching fish:—That sportsman is a fisher of trout.

—**fissure** a deep crack or crevasse in rock, earth, or ice:—In mountain climbing we had to cross several deep fissures.

flair (rhymes with care) a knack or aptitude for doing, selecting, performing, etc.:—John has a flair for doing tricks of magic.

—**flare** a sudden flash of intense light or flame:—That flare in the sky is from a large bonfire celebrating the winning of the football game.

flea (rhymes with be) a tiny black blood-sucking winged insect infesting dogs and cats:—Our dog is covered with fleas.

—**flee** run away from something or someone:—The thief tried to flee from his pursuers.

flew (rhymes with true) past tense of **fly**, soar through the air, travel by

plane:—We flew to Mexico last summer.

—**flu** short for **influenza**, a respiratory disease:—Last week I spent three days in bed with the flu.

—**flue** a large pipe for carrying off smoke from a furnace into the chimney:—If you don't have your flue cleaned regularly, the chimney will smoke.

floc (rhymes with rock) an irregularly shaped piece of material such as wool or smoke:—A floc of wool was placed on the post of the spinning wheel and spun into thread.

—**flock** a group of animals or people cared for by a shepherd:—The priest cares for his flock.

flocks (rhymes with rocks) plural of **flock**, a group:—Flocks of sheep are nibbling the grass in that large pasture.

—**phlox** a common plant in a flower garden. It is formed of clumps of white, red, or purple flowers.

floe (rhymes with go) a large broken piece of ice floating in a river or ocean:—Ice floes retarded the progress of the Hudson River ferry.

—**flow** the forward movement of a running liquid:—In a drought the flow of water from the reservoirs is considerably reduced.

flour (rhymes with sour) the fine powder resulting from grinding cereal or grain:—Bread is made principally from wheat flour.

—**flower** the blossom of a plant or tree:—The rose is the flower of the rosebush.

flow see **floe**

flower see **flour**

flu see **flew**

flue see **flew**

foaled (rhymes with told) past tense of **foal**, give birth to a baby horse:—The mare foaled two colts last year.

—**fold** 1. turn flexible material over on itself so that it takes up less space:—A machine folds newspapers in half before they are placed on sale. 2. a certain group or organization of people:—Barnes is in the Democratic fold.

for (rhymes with door) the common preposition with various meanings:— 1. That book is for Mary (to be given to Mary). 2. Z was substituted for Y (put in place of). 3. When does he come for the garbage? (to collect the garbage). 4. I need a pair of shoes for hiking (to use in hiking). 5. He stopped in a restaurant for he was very hungry (because he was very hungry).

—fore 1. in front, opposite of **hind**:— When Jones became ill, his wife came to the fore and ran his business. 2. a warning cry meaning "look out!" used in golf:—Although I had shouted "fore," the players ahead of us never looked around, and one of them got hit.

—four the number after three and before five.

fore see **for**

foreword (rhymes with bordered) a preface to a book:—The author's publisher wrote a foreword to the book.

—*forward 1. ahead, in front:—At a command the line of soldiers marched forward. 2. send a delivered letter or package to a new or correct address:—We asked the postman to forward all our mail to us at our summer camp. 3. bold, unladylike:— Joan was very forward in asking Leslie to marry her.

fort (rhymes with sort) a strongly walled military enclosure with large guns and resident soldiers:—Much of the world's gold is stored in Fort Knox.

—forte[1] strong point, something one does well:—Playing the violin is certainly not Harry's forte. His practicing is dreadful to listen to.

forte[2] (rhymes with sortie) played very loud, said of music:—The horns played that forte passage in the Beethoven symphony very well.

—forty ten less than fifty.

forth (rhymes with north) ahead or from the inside to the outside:— Christ went forth to preach the gospel. From the cave there came forth a large lion.

—fourth between third and fifth:— Wednesday is the fourth day of the week.

forty see **forte[2]**

forward see **foreword**

foul (rhymes with howl) 1. evil-smelling:—The rotting garbage gave out a foul odor. 2. dirty:—This floor is foul and needs a washing. 3. hateful:—Murder is a foul crime.

—fowl an edible bird such as a duck, chicken, or turkey:—We had a roast fowl and a bottle of wine for dinner.

four see **for**

fourth see **forth**

fowl see **foul**

franc (rhymes with bank) a unit of money used in France:—Our lunch cost us fifteen francs.

—Frank 1. (Cap.) a boy's name. 2. (l.c.) open, plain-spoken:—I was very frank with my new employee and told her she was lazy.

Frances a girl's name

—Francis a boy's name

frank see **franc**

Frank see **franc**

frays (rhymes with days) third person singular of **fray**, wear, become worn, said of cloth:—Constant typing frays the typist's coat-sleeves.

—phrase a grammatical unit of words such as a prepositional or participial phrase:—In the sentence:—Give the book to me—"to me" is a prepositional phrase.

frees (rhymes with bees) third person singular of **free**, set loose, liberate:— The baby-sitter frees Mother for shopping.

—freeze get very cold, solidify or turn to ice:—Water will freeze at 32 degrees Fahrenheit.

—frieze horizontal band of ornamental

sculpture over the pillars of a Greek temple:—Remnants of the frieze of the Parthenon have been preserved.

friar (rhymes with higher) male member of a religious order:—Franciscan friars wear hoods.

—fryer a chicken or similar fowl that is meant to be fried:—I bought a two-pound fryer for our dinner.

frieze see frees

fryer see friar

fur see fir

G

G (rhymes with be, fee) the seventh letter of the alphabet:—There is one g in "gift."

—gee an exclamation of surprise, impatience, or disappointment:—Gee, Mom, do I have to wash the dishes?

gait (rhymes with late) the way an animal or human being walks:—A horse is taught a variety of gaits.

—gate a low door at the entrance or opening of a fence or wall:—The farmer opened the gate and let the cows out of the fenced-in enclosure.

gamble (rhymes with ramble) bet or wager money on cards, horse-races, etc.:—Chris likes to gamble on the horses.

—gambol frolic, run and leap in good spirits:—Lambs like to gambol on the ground in the springtime.

gate see gait

gee see G

gene (rhymes with keen) 1. part of a living cell that determines inheritance of certain traits:—Genes are not affected by acquired characteristics. 2. (Cap.) a boy's name.

—Jean an American girl's name.

gibe (rhymes with bribe) scoff, taunt:—The speaker was intimidated by gibes from the audience.

—jibe match, fit together, agree:—That door and its doorway won't jibe.

gild (rhymes with killed) cover with gold paint:—Every ten years they have to re-gild the spire of their church.

—guild a medieval association of skilled workmen:—Masters, journeymen, and apprentices made up the guild.

gill¹ (rhymes with mill) a liquid measure, one-fourth of a pint:—The cook poured a gill of water into the cake mixture.

—Jill a girl's name.

gilt (rhymes with built) golden or gilded:—A silver-gilt dish is a solid silver dish that has been covered with gold.

—guilt wrongdoing, the fact that one has committed a crime or other wrong:—The jury had to decide the accused's innocence or guilt.

gored (rhymes with lord) past tense of gore, stab or puncture with an animal's horns:—That farmer was badly gored by an ox.

—gourd type of fruit such as a pumpkin, watermelon, etc.: Natives in the tropics make drinking vessels out of gourds.

gorilla (rhymes with vanilla) the largest and strongest of apes:—That zoo has a gorilla in captivity.

—guerrilla a fighter engaged in irregular warfare, using sniping tactics:—The Huks in the Philippines were guerrillas.

gourd see gored

grade (rhymes with spade) 1. sort into categories according to quality, size, etc.:—The farmer grades his eggs into large, medium, and small. 2. class in school:—My son is in the third grade. 3. mark on an exam:—Elsie got a good grade in French last semester.

—grayed past tense of gray, become gray-haired:—Look how Tim has grayed during the past year.

grate (rhymes with late) 1. an iron grille in a stove or furnace used to hold hot coals:—We used to shake the grates in order to dislodge the ashes. 2. rub small pieces of orange or lemon skin off on a metal grater:—Since our cake recipe called for a tablespoonful of grated orange skin, we had to grate an orange.

—**great** very large, important:—A great wind blew down several trees. "Hamlet" is a great play.

grayed see **grade**

grays (rhymes with stays) plural of gray, a color:—That artists paints in grays and blues.

—**graze** 1. chew and eat grass out in pasture, said of cows, horses, and sheep:—Our sheep graze in that meadow. 2. scrape only the surface, make a superficial wound:—A bullet grazed the soldier's arm without greatly hurting him.

grease (rhymes with peace) thick, soft mineral or vegetable substance used for lubrication of a machine or for cooking:—The cook had to clean the grease out of her frying pans. What kind of grease do you use in your car?

—**Greece** the country in southeastern Europe:—Athens is the capital of Greece.

great see **grate**

Greece see **grease**

grill (rhymes with still) to broil meat:— We grilled our steak on an electric range.

—**grille** iron openwork design on a window or door:—We could see inside the house through a grille in the door.

grip (rhymes with lip) a holding or clutching in the hand, a tightening of the hand upon an object:—In crossing the street, the mother held her small child's hand with a firm grip.

—**grippe** influenza:—He has been in bed with the grippe for three days.

grisly (rhymes with frizzly) ghastly, horrible:—The murdered man's body was a grisly sight.

—**grizzly** a large bear:—We shot a grizzly in the woods.

groan (rhymes with bone) utter mournful sounds of distress or pain:—The

cost of his wife's new fur coat made him groan.

—**grown** past participle of **grow**, increase in size:—How those children have grown in the past six months!

guerilla see **gorilla**

guessed (rhymes with best) past tense of **guess** 1. risk or venture an opinion about a fact unknown to the guesser:—From the stranger's very shabby clothes and outstretched hand I guessed he was a beggar. 2. think, plan to:—He said he guessed he'd go shopping tomorrow.

—**guest** a person entertained by his host or one staying at a hotel:—Smith was a summer guest at his son's beach cottage. In August that hotel is full of guests.

guide (rhymes with side) a leader, director:—Our camping guide took us through the woods.

—**guyed** past tense of **guy**, make fun of, ridicule:—Tom's friends guyed him about his sweetheart.

guild see **gild**

guilt see **gilt**

guise (rhymes with wise) dress, appearance:—The angel revealed himself in the guise of a dove.

—**guys** plural of **guy**, a fellow, man:— Two of the guys went on a fishing trip.

guyed see **guide**

guys see **guise**

gym (rhymes with him) short for "gymnasium," a large indoor arena for sports and games:—We played basketball in the college gym.

—**Jim** short for **James**, a man's name.

H

hail (rhymes with fail) 1. small balls of ice that rain from the sky during a thunderstorm:—Yesterday we had hailstones as big as bird's eggs. 2. call out a greeting or salute:—As I was leaving my house, a neighbor who was mowing his lawn hailed me.

3. flag, summon:—I am going to hail a taxi and go downtown.

—hale 1. healthy, in good physical condition:—At seventy that man is as hale and hearty as he was at forty. 2. summon or compel attendance at court:—The police will hale speeders into court.

hair (rhymes with care) protective covering of the human head or of the bodies of some animals:—A blonde has yellow hair.

—hare a rabbit:—We shot a wild hare and had it for supper.

hairy (rhymes with carry) with a lot of hair especially on the arms and legs:—The gorilla is a very hairy animal.

—harry 1. (Cap.) a man's given name. 2. drive out, expel:—The English government used to harry all Catholics out of the country.

hale see hail

hall (rhymes with all) 1. a public or private corridor:—The four rooms of the apartment open out into a long narrow hall. 2. a public room or auditorium:—We heard a wonderful pianist at Town Hall.

—haul 1. drag, pull a heavy load, transport:—The railroads haul coal from the mines to the factories. 2. profit:—Tom made quite a haul on that stock transaction.

halve (rhymes with calve, salve) cut in two or in halves, divide into two equal parts:—Each year those business partners halve expenses and profits.

—have possess something:—I have a new suit.

handmade (rhymes with band-aid) constructed by hand, not machine made, hence usually choice and more expensive:—He pays a hundred dollars a pair for his handmade shoes.

—handmaid a female servant or attendant:—Before the Civil War the Southern lady had a Negro slave as her handmaid.

handsome (rhymes with ransom) 1. good-looking, attractive:—There goes an attractive couple—a beautiful wife and her handsome husband. 2. large, generous:—A handsome gift, anonymously given to our church, will pay for a new organ.

—hansom a horse-drawn, two-wheeled covered carriage:—It was a snowy night and we hired a hansom and were driven around the park.

hangar (rhymes with clangor, rang her) a large tall shed for housing airplanes:—The plane was brought out of the hangar and warmed up before it took off.

—hanger a triangular frame of wood or wire used to suspend clothing from a pole or rack by means of an attached hook:—The dry-cleaning store returned my suit on a hanger.

hansom see handsome

hare see hair

Harry see hairy

hart (rhymes with start) a male deer:—The King shot and killed a hart in the royal forest.

—heart 1. The organ that pumps an animal's blood to his arteries:—Most people have their hearts located on the left side of the chest. 2. The center or chief part:—Radio City is in the heart of Manhattan.

haul see hall

have see halve

hay (rhymes with day) 1. tall grass cut and dried and fed to horses and cattle:—Today farmers cut and bale their hay in one operation.

—hey an exclamation to attract attention:—"Hey! You forgot your change," cried the cashier to the departing customer.

hays (rhymes with days) third person singular of hay, cut tall grass or hay:—Farmer Jones hays all his fields in July.

—haze a slight lack of clearness in the air on a fair day:—During the hot afternoon a gray haze overspread the valley.

heal (rhymes with meal) cure, said of the action of a doctor or of nature itself:—The doctor heals the sick. Tom's deep knife wound will heal very slowly.

—**heel** 1. the end of a person's foot opposite the toes and under the ankle:—I walked so far that I got a blister on my heel. 2. the part of a shoe worn under the wearer's heel:—Women wear high heels to formal parties. 3. (slang) an objectionable or disliked person, one who has done a dishonorable act:—That heel deserted his wife and children and refuses to support them.

—**he'll** contraction of he will:—John is so punctual that I'm sure he'll be on time.

hear (rhymes with near) 1. experience sound sensations:—We like to hear a good concert. 2. find out, learn:—I hear that Smith is going to run for the Senate.

—**here** in this place, opposite of there:—I just saw Sam right here in this room.

heard (rhymes with bird) past tense of hear:—I heard a strange noise in the kitchen last night.

—**herd** a group or crowd of animals or people:—Father Green has a large herd of cows. A herd of autograph seekers beseiged the movie star.

heart see **hart**

he'd (rhymes with seed) contraction of he would or he had:—He'd like to become an air pilot. He'd already had his breakfast by the time I got up.

—**heed** pay attention to, watch, be guided by:—The driver failed to heed the speed-limit sign and was arrested for speeding. Let John heed his parents' advice and save his money.

heel see **heal**

heir see **air**

he'll see **heal**

herd see **heard**

here see **hear**

hew (rhymes with few) cut and fell with an axe:—That woodsman hews many trees each winter.

—**hue** color, shade:—She wore a dress of a light-blue hue.

—**Hugh** a man's first name:—Hugh left his book on the table.

hey see **hay**

hi (rhymes with try) a greeting or welcome, a hello:—Hi there! Are you going my way?

—**hie** hasten, hurry:—At daybreak the hunters hie to the woods.

—**high** 1. tall, opposite of low:—That mountain is very high. 2. expensive:—Peaches are very high when out of season.

hide (rhymes with side) 1. secrete, cover:—The squirrel hides its nuts in a tree. 2. The skin of an animal, raw leather:—The hides of slaughtered steers are sold to tanning or leather-making factories.

—**hied** past tense of hie, hasten:—After school the boys hied themselves to the baseball game.

hie see **hi**

hied see **hide**

high see **hi**

higher (rhymes with buyer) comparative of high:—A is a higher mark than B.

—**hire** employ someone or rent something:—We hired a car and a driver to take us around Ireland.

him (rhymes with dim) objective case of he:—Give the book to him.

—**hymn** a short religious poem or song set to music:—Before the sermon the congregation sang a hymn.

hire see **higher**

hoar (rhymes with door) white, said of frost or hair:—The November ground was covered with hoar frost.

—**whore** a prostitute.

hoard (rhymes with ford) save up and secrete food, money, or other property, store:—A miser hoards his gold.

—horde a large number or great crowd of people, animals, insects, etc.:—Hordes of Christmas shoppers jammed into the stores last December.

hoarse (rhymes with force) said of a person's voice when it is harsh, rough, and indistinct:—After speaking for two hours on the Senate floor, the Senator became hoarse.

—horse the most common beast of burden:—The horse was extensively used to transport people and freight before the motor car displaced it.

hoes (rhymes with goes) plural of hoe, a garden implement used in digging or weeding:—I have to hoe our corn before the weeds get too high.

—hose 1. stockings for women or socks for men:—Mary wears sheer nylon hose. 2. a long flexible rubber or plastic tube used for watering a lawn or garden:—I attached our hose to the water faucet and sprinkled the grass.

hole (rhymes with goal) an opening in a piece of wood, metal, cloth or other material, also a scooped-out depression in the ground:—There are so many of my socks that have holes that I am buying some new pairs.

—whole complete:—He told me the whole story of his life.

holy (rhymes with lowly) sacred, sanctified:—A saint is a holy man.

—wholly completely:—His money is wholly gone.

horde see hoard

horse see hoarse

hose see hoes

hostel (rhymes with nostril) an inn or overnight shelter for hikers:—There are many youth hostels all over Europe.

—hostile unfriendly, threatening, said of an enemy:—Hostile airplanes dropped bombs on the defenseless city.

hour (rhymes with tower) sixty minutes:—Our plane leaves within the hour.

—our (stressed) possessive of we:—Come over and hear our new records. (See also are—our for unstressed our)

hue see hew

Hugh see hew

humerus (rhymes with tumerous) one of the two arm bones extending from shoulder to elbow:—Mary slipped on the ice and fractured her humerus.

—humorous funny, laughable:—The after-dinner speaker told a humorous story.

hymn see him

I

I see aye

idle (rhymes with tidal) not working, said of a person who is unemployed or who otherwise does nothing useful either because he is lazy or because he can't work or find employment; also said of a machine that is not operating:—John is idle and won't do his homework. Factory shutdowns made many workers idle for several weeks.

—idol 1. a three-dimensional representation of a god:—The Chinese used to worship idols. 2. a person that others reverence and look up to:—Johnny's idol is baseball's current star pitcher.

I'll see aisle

illusion see allusion

in (rhymes with tin) preposition meaning into, inside:—Let's go in the house where it's warmer.

—inn a small country hotel:—We stopped at a very good inn just off the parkway.

indict (rhymes with incite) the bringing of a formal charge or accusation against a criminal suspect by a grand jury:—The jury is expected to indict the captured car thief for grand larceny.

—indite write literature, especially poetry or a letter:—I indite a letter to Mother every Sunday.

inn see in

instance an example:—Give me just one instance of that loafer ever doing any work.

—*instants plural of instant, a moment:—I started a fire in the fireplace and several instants afterwards I had a blazing pile of logs.

insure see ensure

intense (rhymes with dispense) very concentrated:—Last summer's heat was intense.

—*intents (rhymes with in rents) plural of intent, purpose:—The intents of both those criminals were identical—to rob a bank.

intercession pleading for assistance or forgiveness by one person in behalf of another:—The theme of the sermon was Christ's intercession in behalf of sinful men.

—intersession the period between the three regular university academic terms:—During the June intersession our teacher went abroad.

invade (rhymes with been made) rush into a place and seize property or persons, trespass:—The Germans had planned to invade Belgium before 1914. Hordes of tourists will invade France this summer.

—inveighed past tense of inveigh, talk against, criticise, condemn:—The Dean of the college inveighed against student riots in the dormitories.

isle see aisle

islet see eyelet

its (rhymes with hits) adjective denoting possession by animals or inanimate objects:—That cat has hurt its paw. That chair has lost one of its legs.

—it's contraction of it is:—It's warm out tonight.

J

J (rhymes with may) the tenth letter of the alphabet:—J comes before K.

—jay a type of bird such as the blue-jay, also (Cap.) a man's first name or a surname.

jam (rhymes with ham) 1. fruit preserves:—We like strawberry jam very much. 2. a clogged mass of cars, logs, etc. that impede traffic or other movement:—A traffic jam held us up for two hours beyond our regular schedule. The loggers had to break up a log jam on the river.

—jamb the side next to a door on which the door hinges:—To remove the door we had to unscrew the hinges from the jamb.

jay see J

Jean see gene

jewels (rhymes with fuels) plural of jewel, a precious stone such as a diamond, etc.:—She wore a pearl necklace with contrasting jewels in her hair.

—Jules a boy's first name.

jibe see gibe

Jill see gill¹

Jim see gym

jinks (rhymes with sinks) foolery, pranks, entertainment:—There were many high jinks at the Valentine party.

—jinx something that spoils a plan, a party, or other occasion:—Rain put the jinx on our projected outdoor picnic.

Joan's (rhymes with bones) possessive form of Joan, a girl's name:—Do you know Joan's telephone number?

—Jones a surname:—John Jones married Joan Smith.

Jules see jewels

K

kernel see colonel

khaki see cocky

kill (rhymes with fill) 1. murder, slaughter:—God saw Cain kill his brother Abel. 2. defeat, ruin:—The majority are expected to kill the housing bill submitted to Congress.

—kiln an oven in which clay products such as dishes, etc. are fired:—Temperatures must be very high in a kiln.

knave (rhymes with save) 1. a tricky, deceitful wrongdoer:—A knave proposed marriage to her and then ran off with all her money. 2. a face card sometimes called the jack:—I played my knave of hearts and won the trick.

—**nave** the large rectangular front interior of a cathedral starting west and running east to the transepts:—The worshippers sit in the nave during a service.

knead (rhymes with speed) squeeze and pound dough in breadmaking:—Mother used to knead her bread before baking it.

—**need** 1. have to have, have a use for, require:—I need a new pack of razor blades. 2. poverty:—That unemployed worker's family is in great need.

knell (rhymes with sell). 1. the slow tolling or ringing of a bell at a death or funeral service:—The knell of the cathedral bells announced the death of the nation's king. 2. the end or loss of something:—The stock market crash sounded the knell of our profits.

—**Nell** a girl's name, short for Helen:—Little Nell is a famous character in Dickens' novel "The Old Curiosity Shop."

knew (rhymes with do, sue) past tense of know, understand, have information about:—I knew the answers to the questions put by the teacher.

—**new** recent, not old:—January first ushers in the new year.

knight (rhymes with light) a medieval warrior that wore armour and rode on a horse:—Sir Galahad was a famous knight.

—**night** opposite of day, a time of darkness:—It gets dark at night.

knot (rhymes with lot) the fastening made by tying two pieces or ends of string, cord, etc. together:—I wear one knot in my necktie. Boy scouts, sailors, and surgeons must learn how to tie knots.

—**not** negative adverb:—I'm not finished with that book yet.

know (rhymes with go) 1. understand, have intelligence or information about:—I know how many ounces there are in a pound. 2. be acquainted with a person:—Yes, I know Sally Blair.

—**no** 1. opposite of yes:—No, I don't know how old Mrs. Pierce is. 2. not any:—I have no children.

knows (rhymes with goes) third person singular of know, understand or have information about:—John knows how to broil steak.

—**noes** plural of no:—There were five ayes and three noes in the vote for the new chairman.

—**nose** the organ of smell:—That homely girl has a rather long nose.

L

lacks (rhymes with sacks) third person singular of lack, be without something:—John lacks courage to fight for his rights.

—**lax** careless, slack:—Barry is very lax about getting to work on time.

lade (rhymes with fade) load merchandise on a truck or ship:—That machine is used to lade coal onto the ship.

—**laid** past tense of lay, put or place:—I laid the pencil on the desk.

lain (rhymes with brain) past participle of lie, recline:—Every day this week I have lain down for a rest after lunch.

—**lane** a small path, also a marked path for automobiles on a highway:—A winding lane led through the fields to the woods. We drove most of the way in the outer lane of the parkway.

Lapps (rhymes with caps) native of Lapland.

—**laps** plural of **lap** 1. That part of the human anatomy between the knees and the stomach when one is sitting down:—The mothers held their babies in their laps. 2. lick with the tongue:—The cat laps up all the milk in her dish. 3. extend over on to another object:—Each board in the walls of that house laps over another board. 4. The complete circuit of a race track:—The horses are now on the final laps of the track.

—**lapse** a break in a good habit or a failing in physical or mental power:—Although George swore off whisky last year, he has had a lapse or two. Grandma suffers from a lapse of memory.

lay (rhymes with say) put or place:—I always lay my books on my desk.

—**lei** Hawaiian wreath or necklace of flowers used for personal adornment:—When the tourists arrived in Hawaii, each was presented with a beautiful lei.

lays (rhymes with days) third person plural of **lay**, put or place:—He lays his watch on his dresser before he goes to bed.

—**laze** loaf, take it easy:—Last summer we would laze on the beach all afternoon.

lax see **lacks**

laze see **lays**

lea (rhymes with be) a grassy field:—There are cattle grazing on the green lea.

—**lee** 1. that side of a boat that is sheltered from the wind:—We moved over to the lee side of the boat to escape getting wet. 2. (Cap.) a surname or given name.

leach (rhymes with teach) soak a mineral out of ashes:—Soap-makers leach potassium salts out of wood ashes.

—**leech** 1. a bloodsucking insect:—Physicians used to apply leeches to patients' arms and legs. 2. a worthless person who drains vitality out of a victim by exacting money or attention:—That man could save money if it weren't for those leeches of idle brothers whom he supports.

lead² (rhymes with bed) the common heavy, dull, soft metal:—Lead pipes are often used by plumbers.

—**led** past tense of **lead**¹, conduct:—Our guide led us hunters through the woods.

leaf (rhymes with thief) the green foliage of a tree or plant:—Lettuce has a green leaf.

—**lief** willingly:—I'd as lief go without a watch as pay a big price for one.

leak (rhymes with Greek) escape of gas, liquid, or solid from a container:—Our thermos bottle started to leak, so we had to buy a new one.

—**leek** a small onion with green shoots:—There were leeks in our salad.

lean (rhymes with clean) 1. brace oneself against:—He usually leans against the mailbox while waiting for a bus. 2. thin, not fat:—He is very lean, but his wife is plump. Lean bacon has little fat.

—**lien** a creditor's legal property right in his debtor's possessions:—John's creditors have a lien on his new car.

leant (rhymes with sent, bent) alternative past participle of **lean**, support oneself against or support something against:—The old man leant on his two canes.

—**lent** 1. past tense of **lend**, transfer possession of an object temporarily:—Last month I lent my car to Frank, and now he wants to borrow it again. 2. (Cap.) the fasting season preceding Easter Sunday:—Mary has sworn off candy for Lent.

leased (rhymes with beast) past tense of **lease**, rent property to a tenant or from a landlord:—The doctor leased a suite of offices on the ground floor of an apartment house.

—**least** the smallest amount or degree:—I don't want to go to the movies in the least. Give me the least expensive cut of beef.

led see **lead**²

lee see **lea**
leech see **leach**
leek see **leak**
lei see **lay**
lends (rhymes with sends) third person singular of **lend**, advance money or property to another temporarily:—That bank lends money at six percent.
—***lens** (rhymes with men's) optical glass:—My camera has an expensive lens.
lent see **leant**
lessen (rhymes with wesson) make smaller, reduce in degree:—Drugs will lessen his pain.
—**lesson** what one is taught in class or elsewhere, also one's class assignment:—Today we had a lesson on the strong verb in English.
levee (rhymes with heavy) an earthen or other kind of wall or bank to hold back a rising river:—There are many levees along the flood banks of the Mississippi.
—**levy²** tax:—There is a three-percent levy on all restaurant checks in that state.
liable (rhymes with pliable) 1. be legally responsible for:—A father is liable for the debts of his children who are under-age.
—***libel** (rhymes with Bible) writing or printing an untruth about another person that tends to injure him:—When the local newspaper printed an article stating that Doctor Smith operated on a patient while he, the surgeon, was drunk, the Doctor sued the paper for libel.
liar (rhymes with wire, tire) one who tells fibs or untruths or lies:—The two elders who lusted after Susannah were proved to be liars.
—**lyre** a stringed instrument smaller than a harp:—The Greek poets often played the lyre.
libel see **liable**
lie (rhymes with try) 1. recline:—It is better to lie on a mattress than on

the floor. 2. tell an untruth:—When John's father found out that John had told his mother a lie, he punished John.
—**lye** a strong alkaline chemical used in cleaning wood, porcelain, etc. and which is also used in soap-making.
lief see **leaf**
lien see **lean**
lightening (rhymes with frightening) making lighter or less heavy a load by removing some of the goods or freight:—Some of the cargo was thrown overboard thus lightening the storm-tossed ship a great deal.
—***lightning** an electrical discharge from the clouds:—That tree was split in two by the lightning.
lo (rhymes with go) an exclamation meaning observe, notice:—John told me he was not going to the party, but lo and behold when we arrived, he was already there.
—**low** 1. not high:—She is short and likes to sit in a low chair. 2. disgraceful:—That was a low trick to steal money from a six-year-old. 3. moan like a cow:—We heard the sick cow low all night.
load (rhymes with code) a burden, cargo or freight:—That truck carries a load of sand.
—**lode** a vein of valuable metal in a mine:—The Comstock Lode was a famous silver mine in the West.
—**lowed** past tense of **low**, make the moaning sound that a cow makes:—The hungry cows lowed in the pasture.
loan (rhymes with bone) 1. temporary transfer of money or other property for which interest is often charged:—I asked for a loan on my house in order to pay my doctor's bills. 2. as a verb used in the same way as **lend**:—Will you loan me your power mower for the day?
—**lone** alone, unaccompanied:—George is a lone wolf; he never goes out with anybody.

locks (rhymes with box) 1. plural of lock, a fastener to a door, etc.:—We have double locks on our front door. 2. the human hair:—At fifty he had snowy locks.

—lox a smoked fish regarded as a delicacy:—For a snack we served lox and bagels.

lode see load

lone see loan

loot (rhymes with boot) booty or stolen property:—With a large bag of loot the robbers left the house that they had broken into.

—lute a medieval stringed instrument:—Queen Elizabeth I is said to have played the lute.

lore (rhymes with core) information about the woods, streams, etc. handed down from primitive times:—Boy Scouts learn lots about the lore of the woods.

—*lower 1. comparative of low, opposite of high:—Bess is in a lower class than I am and graduates a year later. 2. a lower berth or bed on a train:—I couldn't get a lower so I got an upper on the Chicago train.

low see lo

lowed see load

lower see lore

lox see locks

lumbar (rhymes with number) pertaining to one's back:—The spine is in the lumbar region.

—lumber 1. wooden boards, etc.: I bought the flooring in a lumber yard. 2. walk clumsily:—The keeper placed food in the big brown bear's cage and watched him lumber up to it.

lute see loot

lye see lie

lyre see liar

M

made (rhymes with fade) past tense of make, manufacture, etc.:—Father made Mother a sewing table.

—maid 1. a young girl:—The way of a man with a maid is proverbial. 2. a female household servant:—The Masons have a maid who comes in five days a week.

mail (rhymes with nail) postal matter:—I received two letters and a package in the mail, but there was no mail for my friend.

—male opposite of female, a boy or man:—Football is a game played by males.

main (rhymes with train) chief:—The main reason I want to go to Europe is to see the museums.

—Maine the most northeastern state in the United States:—Augusta is the capital of Maine.

—mane the thick growth of hair on a horse's neck:—Feeling that he was slipping, the rider grasped the horse's mane.

maize (rhymes with days) Indian sweet-corn or corn on the cob:—Europeans discovered maize in America.

—May's possessive of May, the fifth month:—May's flowers are early ones.

—maze a labyrinth:—In Boston we got lost in the maze of irregularly shaped streets.

male see mail

mall (rhymes with tall) a wide promenade in a park:—Concerts are given on the mall in Central Park.

—maul scratch, use roughly, beat:—At the zoo the lions mauled their keeper.

mane see main

manner (rhymes with banner) way, attitude, bearing:—There was something in the sailor's manner which displeased me.

—manor a large section of privately held land in the British countryside:—The baronet lives in the manor house on his manor.

mantel (rhymes with cantle) a high shelf over a fireplace:—The clock stood on the mantel.

—mantle an outdoor garment such as a

coat or cloak:—Mary wore a blue mantle outdoors during the winter weather.

marks (rhymes with parks) plural of mark, a drawn line or smudge:—The neighbor's baby left marks all over our wallpaper.

—**Marx** surname of a famous writer on socialism or communism.

marry (rhymes with carry) wed:—John is going to marry Jane.

—**Mary** a girl's name.

—**merry** happy, joyous:—A merry Christmas to you.

marshall (rhymes with partial) 1. a high military officer:—Napoleon had several marshalls under him. 2. a federal court official:—A federal marshall arrested the income-tax dodger. 3. assemble, superintend:—The political candidate must marshall all his supporters for the campaign.

—**martial** warlike:—The band played a martial tune.

Marx see **marks**

Mary see **marry**

mask (rhymes with task) a shaped cloth or other fabric worn over part or all of the face to disguise the wearer:—At the masked ball each of us wore a mask.

—**masque** a dance or festival where all attending wear masks:—The Mardi Gras in New Orleans is like a masque.

massed (rhymes with fast) past tense of mass, gather in a closely packed crowd:—The worshippers massed together in the Square to watch the Pope address them from the balcony.

—**mast** the tall, upright pole on a sailing vessel or elsewhere which is used to carry the sails or for other purposes:—In the storm the ship's main mast broke. There is a broadcasting mast atop the Empire State Building.

maul see **mall**

May's see **maize**

maze see **maize**

me (rhymes with tree) objective case of the pronoun I:—Whatever suits you suits me.

—**mi** the third note in the musical solfège scale:—Do, re, mi, fa, sol, etc.

mead (rhymes with feed) grassy meadow:—There were lovely green meads around the old manor house.

—**meed** a reward:—A kiss was his meed for helping Mary sweep the kitchen.

mean (rhymes with green) 1. signify:—"Bruder" means "brother" in English. What does Jack's silence mean? 2. unpleasant to another:—He was so mean to his own son that the latter ran away from home. 3. intend:—I mean to pass this course with an A. 4. shabby:—He lives in a mean rooming house.

—**mien** a person's bearing or presence, the way he carries himself:—The King was of royal mien.

meat (rhymes with heat) animal flesh or the edible inside of a nut:—A butcher shop is also called a meat market.

—**meet.** 1. join another person or persons:—I'll meet you at the drugstore in fifteen minutes. 2. undergo, experience:—Enroute to Boston we met with an accident. He meets all his difficulties with good humour.

—**mete** pay out, measure out as a punishment:—The judge is expected to mete out a heavy sentence to the convicted thief.

meatier (rhymes with sleetier) comparative meaning fuller of meat:—I find this chop meatier than the one I cooked last week.

—**meteor** a falling star:—We saw a brilliant meteor drop from the sky last night.

medal (rhymes with pedal) an award or decoration of honor made of an engraved metal disk with a ribbon attached:—The President pinned a medal on the breast of the courageous soldier.

—**meddle** interfere with another person or with his business or property:—Stop meddling with my watch! Put it down!

meed see **mead**

meet see **meat**

meeter (rhymes with liter) better, more fitting:—It is meeter that he ask her for a date than that she ask him.

—**meter** 1. a unit of measurement:—A meter is one-tenth of a decameter. 2. time value of music:—That waltz is written in ¾ meter. 3. an instrument for measuring the consumer's use of gas, water, or electricity:—The Edison Company reads our meter every month.

merry see **marry, Mary**

metal (rhymes with settle) one of the elements such as iron, gold, or silver, etc.:—Gold is a very heavy metal.

—**mettle** courage, prowess, as regards a person's intellectual or physical disposition:—That lawyer faces opposing counsel of mettle.

mete see **meat**

meteor see **meatier**

meter see **meeter**

mettle see **metal**

mewl (rhymes with fuel) make a complaining cry such as a baby or small child does:—I can't bear hearing that youngster mewl all night.

—**mule** 1. a beast of burden, a cross between a horse and a jackass:—A team of mules pulled the cultivator. 2. a kind of slipper without toes or heels:—She wears blue silk mules around the house.

mews (rhymes with news) 1. third person singular of mew, cry like a cat:—When our cat mews, it wants some milk. 2. a row of carriage or horse stables which are today usually converted into apartments:—There are many mews in London.

—**muse** 1. wonder or speculate about something:—From time to time he would muse on his past failures. 2.

a creative artist's inspiration:—Inspired by the muse, Keats wrote great poetry.

mi see **me**

mien see **mean**

might (rhymes with white) 1. power:—The might of the Allies defeated Germany. 2. past tense of **may**:—I asked him if I might help him with his homework.

—**mite** 1. a small person or child:—We enjoyed visiting the kindergarten and watching a little mite playing in the sandbox. 2. a small contribution to charity or the church:—The widow's mite was commended by Christ.

mince (rhymes with since) 1. cut meat, etc. into very small pieces:—Mince pie is made of mince-meat. 2. speak politely rather than frankly:—Not to mince words that fellow is a scoundrel.

—**mints*** (rhymes with hints) plural of **mint** 1. a spearmint or peppermint flavor used in drinks, gum, and candy, also candy so flavored:—We ate after-dinner mints with our coffee. 2. plural of mint, a factory where coins are manufactured:—Those fresh shiny quarters have just come from one of the Government mints.

mind (rhymes with kind) 1. the seat of the intelligence, the brain:—That scholar has a good mind. 2. intention:—I have a good mind to vacuum the rugs. 3. object to:—Would you mind my shutting the windows? 4. obey:—That spoiled child doesn't mind his parents. 5. pay attention to, heed:—Don't mind what he says about you; he's only jealous.

—**mined** past tense of mine, dig for ore:—In the old days they mined for iron in northern New Jersey.

miner (rhymes with liner) a man who digs for coal, iron, gold, and other metals:—That miner uses a machine to cut the coal out of an underground seam.

—**minor** 1. opposite of **major:**—That political candidate's religion is a minor issue. 2. a person under 21 and hence under legal age:—Beer may not be sold to a minor in New Jersey. 3. a scale or chord in music that is not a major chord or scale:—That folk-song is in a minor key.

minks (rhymes with sinks) plural of **mink,** a small valuable fur-bearing animal, also the fur itself:—Her coat is made of minks' fur.

—**minx** a lively, saucy girl:—He tried to kiss the flirtatious girl, but the minx slipped out of his grasp.

minor see **miner**

mints see **mince**

minx see **minks**

missal (rhymes with bristle) a book of prayers and church services or masses: —Eleanor always takes her missal with her to Sunday mass.

—**missile** a projectile, an object hurled as a weapon:—In fighting, the small boys used stones as missiles.

missed (rhymes with list) past tense of **miss:**—1. fail to reach or connect with:—I missed my friend at the airport because her plane was two hours late and I couldn't stay. 2. feel lonesome without:—When Elsie was first married, she missed her mother dreadfully.

—**mist** air saturated with fine droplets of water like a fog:—In the late afternoon the mist rolled inshore from the sea.

misses (rhymes with kisses) two or more unmarried ladies:—The Misses Jones and their parents visited France last summer.

—**Mrs.** title of a married woman:—Mrs. Jones was formerly Miss Baker.

missile see **missal**

mist see **missed**

mite see **might**

moan (rhymes with bone) a deep sound of pain:—The sick man suffered all night, and his moans awakened the other patients.

—**mown** past participle of **mow,** cut the grass:—We had to have our lawn mown.

moat (rhymes with boat) deep water-filled ditch encircling a castle:—A drawbridge stretched across the moat.

—**mote** a very small particle like a grain of dust:—A mote which got in my eye enflamed it.

mode (rhymes with code) fashion, way, manner:—Long skirts were the mode a few years ago.

—**mowed** past tense of **mow,** cut grass: —Father mowed the grass with his power mower.

mood (rhymes with rude) a person's disposition or feelings at a particular time:—Sam has been in an ugly mood ever since he smashed his car.

—**mooed** past tense of **moo,** make a sound like a cow:—When I started to pat the cow, she mooed at me.

moor (rhymes with tour) 1. (Cap.) a native of Morocco:—The Moors invaded Spain in the thirteenth century. 2. a desolate plain in Scotland: —Shooting on a Scottish moor in the fall is very popular. 3. fasten or tie up a boat to a pier or dock:—We usually moor our sailboat to our own dock.

—*****more** comparative of **much:**—He has more money than you have.

moose (rhymes with noose) an animal similar to but larger than a deer, with prominent antlers:—On a hunting trip Father shot a bull moose.

—**mousse** a frozen dessert made with heavy cream:—We had coffee mousse for dessert.

more see **moor**

morning (rhymes with warning) the first or earlier part of the day:—This morning we had bacon and eggs for breakfast.

—**mourning** expression of sorrow for another's death, often expressed by the wearing of dark clothes:—Mrs.

Grace is in mourning for her late husband.

mote see **moat**

mourning see **morning**

mousse see **moose**

mowed see **mode**

mown see **moan**

Mrs. see **misses**

mule see **mewl**

muse see **mews**

mussed (rhymes with dust) past tense of muss, disorder, rumple:—Alice got angry when her boy-friend mussed her hair.

—**must** 1. auxiliary verb meaning have to:—I must pay my bills. 2. a damp, unpleasant musty smell:—The cellar smelled of must.

mustard (rhymes with custard) a sharp yellow spice in powdered or paste form:—We spread mustard on our ham sandwich.

—**mustered** past tense of muster, assemble troops in an army:—The Germans mustered a hundred thousand infantry.

N

naval (rhymes with Wavell) pertaining to a navy or group of ships:—We saw several naval aircraft carriers.

—**navel** 1. the belly button:—The newborn baby was joined to his mother at the navel. 2. also a type of orange with a navel:—Florida navels are now on sale.

nave see **knave**

navel see **naval**

nay (rhymes with say) no:—Nay, I can't join you at dinner. There were more nays than yeas, so the proposed bill didn't pass in Congress.

—**née** born:—Mrs. Robert White, née Alice Jones, is abroad.

—**neigh** the sound a horse makes:—The neigh of that horse startled me.

need see **knead**

neigh see **nay**

Nell see **knell**

new see **knew**

Nice[1] (rhymes with geese, cease) a city in Southern France

—**niece** the daughter of one's brother or sister:—My only niece is my brother's youngest child.

night see **knight**

no see **know**

noes see **knows**

none (rhymes with run) not any:—None of us knows how to speak Russian.

—**nun** a sister, a female member of a church order:—Nuns teach in the Catholic schools.

nose see **knows**

not see **knot**

nun see **none**

O

O (rhymes with go) an exclamation of address:—O Moon, shine on your people.

—**oh** an exclamation expressing surprise, resentment, etc.:—Oh, I forgot to do your errand.

—**owe** be obligated to, or be in debt to another for something:—I owe the grocer a large bill. We owe our excellent speaker a vote of thanks.

oar (rhymes with store) a pole bladed at one end usually used in pairs to propel a small boat:—While rowing on the lake, I broke an oar.

—**o'er** contraction of over:—The birds flew o'er the lake at dusk.

—**or** word expressing alternation:—John is thirty or thirty-one years old.

—**ore** an unrefined mineral:—Those mountains are rich in iron ore.

ode (rhymes with code) a poem of praise:—That poet wrote an ode to his mistress.

—**oh'd** past tense of oh, express wonder at:—Mrs. Green's friends oh'd and ah'd at her new baby.

—**owed** past tense of owe, be indebted to:—Since I owed the druggist ten dollars, I decided to pay him.

o'er see **oar**

offal see **awful**

oh see **O**

oh'd see **ode**

omit see **emit**

one (rhymes with gun) a single person or unit:—The baby is one year old. If you have an extra cigarette, I'd like one.

—won past tense of win, defeat an opponent in a game or sport:—I played tennis with Don and he won.

oral see **aural**

or see **oar**

ore see **oar**

ought see **aught**

our see **are, hour**

overdo (rhymes with drove her to) do more than is proper, comfortable, or safe:—John mustn't play basketball every night in the week. I don't want him to overdo.

—overdue past the due or agreed day, said of bills long unpaid:—On July first I received a notice that my telephone bill was three months overdue.

overseas (rhymes with Dover trees) abroad:—During the last war the United States sent many soldiers overseas to Europe and Asia.

—oversees third person singular of oversee, direct, superintend:—Smith's son is in charge of the family business, but Smith himself oversees most of the important aspects of it.

owe see **O**

owed see **ode**

ox-eyed (rhymes with dockside) having large soft brown eyes like those of an ox:—The medical student fell in love with a petite ox-eyed nurse.

—oxide a chemical compound containing oxygen:—Rust is an oxide of **iron.**

P

P (rhymes with he) the 16th letter of the alphabet:—There is one p in the word "hope."

—pea a green round vegetable found in pea pods:—We had fresh green peas with our roast lamb.

paced (rhymes with taste) past tense of pace, set a speed for others to keep up with:—On the athlete's daily run along the country road he was paced by his trainer in a car.

—paste a mixture of flour and water used to make paper adhere or stick to other paper:—We used paste to fasten our newspaper clippings in a scrapbook.

packed (rhymes with tracked) past tense of pack, fill a box or suitcase:—We are all packed and ready for our trip to Europe.

—pact an agreement, treaty:—The two friendly nations made a pact of peace.

pail (rhymes with fail) a large circular wooden or metal vessel with a round wire handle:—I carried a pail of water from the spring into the house.

—pale of very light color, nearly white:—When the stranger seized her, the young girl turned pale with fright.

pain (rhymes with gain) an ache or hurting sensation:—That veteran frequently suffers pain from an old leg wound.

—pane a section of glass in a door or window:—Today I washed every pane in our windows.

pair (rhymes with care) a set of two items that match or complement each other such as a pair of gloves, shoes, etc.:—I have a pair of tickets to the Broadway musical hit.

—pare 1. trim with a knife or scissors:—I must pare my nails; they are too long. 2. remove the skins of fruit or vegetables with a knife:—I pared the potatoes and boiled them.

—pear the familiar pyramidically rounded fruit:—We had pear salad for lunch.

palate (rhymes with ballot) 1. the roof of the mouth:—The soft palate lies beyond the hard palate. 2. one's sense of taste:—Lobsters always tempt Stephen's palate.

—palette a round thin board held in the left hand by an artist on which he mixes his paints:—That artist has sixteen different kinds of colors on his palette.

pale see pail

palette see palate

pall (rhymes with hall) 1. become less intense or interesting:—After eating a third piece of pie, John felt his appetite begin to pall. 2. a dark mist or cloud:—A pall of smoke hung over the city all afternoon. 3. The bed a dead person lies on:—Flowers decorated the pall on which lay the deceased in his casket.

—Paul à boy's name.

—pawl a mechanical catch to prevent the reverse motion of a gear.

pane see pain

pare see pair

parish (rhymes with garish) a geographical division containing one church and one priest:—There are two thousand people in our parish.

—perish die:—Without protective coverings Arctic explorers would perish from the cold.

passed (rhymes with last) past tense of pass, go by or ahead of someone or something:—The faster car passed the slower one.

—past 1. the time before the present:— In the past we used to listen to the radio more than we do today. 2. after, beyond:—It is half-past six. That bill is way past due. 3. the past tense:—"She ran" is the past of "She runs."

paste see paced

patience (rhymes with rations) ability to act calmly or endure suffering, annoyance or disappointment:—That teacher's patience with her backward pupils is amazing.

—*patients a physician's clients, sick persons under a doctor's care and often in a hospital:—That doctor sees his office patients every morning.

Paul see pall

pause (rhymes with laws) a break or interruption in work, talk, music, etc.:—During a pause in the rehearsal, the director talked with the producers of the play.

—paws the feet of an animal such as a dog, cat, etc.:—That dog bruised one of its paws on a stone.

pawl see pall

paws see pause

pea see P

peace (rhymes with lease, geese) 1. opposite of war:—After the decisive battle, the defeated nation sued for peace. 2 calmness, quiet:—Mrs. Jones sent her three children to camp so she could have some peace around the house.

—piece 1. a part of the whole:—Would you like a piece of this delicious cake? 2. an article of china, furniture, etc.:—That sofa is a nice old piece. 3. a musical composition:—A sonata is a formal piano piece.

peak (rhymes with seek) top point, summit:—Mt. McKinley is the highest peak in North America.

—peek a glance from a hidden position, a stolen look at someone or something:—On Christmas Eve the children wanted a peek at Santa Claus.

—pique 1. a wound to one's vanity or one's feelings, resentment:—Rob refused the offer of a vice-presidency out of pique for not being offered the presidency. 2. excite, stimulate:— The delivery of several large packages to my next-door neighbor always piques my curiosity.

peal (rhymes with feel) give out the deep sound of a large ringing bell:— After the great victory the church bells of London began to peal joyously.

—peel 1. take off the outer skin of a potato, orange, peach, etc.:—Mother said to peel the potatoes and put them on the stove to boil.

pean (rhymes with Leon) a hymn of praise:—At festivals the ancient Greeks sang peans to their gods.

—**peon** a Spanish-American laborer:— In Mexico the peons work on farms.

pear see **pair**

pearl (rhymes with girl) a jewel made inside an oyster:—Mary wore a string of imitation pearls around her neck.

—**purl** 1. a knitting stitch:—The direction for the sweater was: knit one, purl two. 2. the murmuring sound of a small stream of water:—We sleep beside a purling brook.

peat (rhymes with heat) earth or turf cut and used for fuel:—The Irish dig up peat and burn it in their stoves.

—**Pete** short for **Peter**, a boy's name.

pedal (rhymes with medal) the foot-operated part of a machine:—When I wanted to stop the car, I stepped on the brake pedal. Our grand piano has three pedals.

—**peddle** sell merchandise from house to house or from a pushcart:—In the summer that college boy peddles brushes from door to door.

peek see **peak**

peel see **peal**

peer (rhymes with near) 1. a titled citizen such as a duke, earl, etc.:—Last summer the British queen created twelve new peers. 2. an equal:—No one is that champion's peer at chess. 3. look at nearsightedly:—The receptionist peered at her caller over her glasses.

—**pier** a long dock or causeway running out to sea at right angles to the land: —Helped by tugs, the great ocean liner was finally moored to her pier.

pend (rhymes with lend) remain unsettled, await a decision:—Many proposed laws pend the action of Congress.

—**penned** past tense of **pen**, write:—I penned a short note to Amy thanking her for her gift.

pendant (rhymes with attendant) a necklace or jeweled charm hanging from a woman's neck:—She wore a pendant of diamonds.

—**pendent** hanging, suspended:—She wore a necklace with a pendent ruby.

penned see **pend**

peon see **pean**

Percy (rhymes with mercy) a boy's name.

—**pursy** fat or short-winded from being fat:—Her husband is rather pursy.

perish see **parish**

pervade (rhymes with surveyed) run through, permeate:—The smell of cooking will pervade the living-room unless the kitchen door is closed.

—**purveyed** past tense of **purvey**, supply or secure provisions for:—The food for that banquet was purveyed by Macy's.

Pete see **peat**

petit (rhymes with Betty) small, said of juries in the lower or minor courts:—Holmes was summoned to serve on a petit jury.

—**petty** insignificant, small, mean, relatively unimportant:—It was very petty of George to deny his hard-working wife a new dress. At the office we always keep twenty dollars in petty cash available.

phase see **faze**

phew see **few**

phial see **file**

Phil see **fill**

phile see **file**

Philip see **fillip**

philtre see **filter**

phlox see **flocks**

phrase see **frays**

pi (rhymes with cry) 1. the sixteenth letter of the Greek alphabet. 2. the number 3.1416.

—**pie** the popular American pastry dessert:—I like apple pie à la mode.

pidgin (rhymes with bridge in, smidgen) business language used by Chinese merchants and foreigners:— We used to communicate with that Chinese dealer in pidgin English.

—**pigeon** a dove:—Pigeons were flying all around the large city hall.

pie see pi

piece see peace

pier see peer

pigeon see pidgin

Pilate (rhymes with file it) the Roman official who delivered Christ to his crucifiers.

—**pilot** the guider of a ship or plane:— That transcontinental plane carries two pilots and a navigator.

pique see peak

plain (rhymes with gain) 1. unadorned, simple:—That boarding house serves good plain food. She wore a plain, untrimmed dress. 2. a large, flat area: —The plains in the western part of the United States stretch out as far a eye can see. 3. not pretty:—Margaret is a very plain girl.

—**plane** 1. a flat surface:—Elementary geometry is called plane geometry. 2. an aeroplane:—We took the midnight plane to Lisbon. 3. a tool that shaves wood or metal:—With his plane the carpenter shaved off some of the door so that it would close easily.

plaintiff the person bringing a lawsuit against a defendant:—The injured automobile driver was the plantiff in the negligence suit.

—***plaintive** arousing pity, mournful:— The suffering child asked for her nurse in a plaintive voice.

plait (rhymes with late) twisted strands of hair, a braid:—Mary wore her hair in plaits.

—**plate** 1. a flat dish, flat tableware:— They set the table with imported dinner plates. 2. a denture:—He wears an upper plate. 3. with a metallic covering:—Those knives and forks are of silver plate.

plane see plain

plate see plait

pleas (rhymes with trees) plural of plea, a request or supplication:—The judge ignored the murderer's pleas for mercy.

—**please** 1. be appealing or ingratiating to another:—His son pleased him by getting good marks in college. Good movies please us all. 2. an expression of politeness in requesting something:—Please pass the pepper.

plum (rhymes with gum) the stone fruit of a plum tree:—We served plum pie for dessert.

—**plumb** straight, not crooked:—A plumb line is always used in laying up brick walls.

Poe's (rhymes with goes) possessive form of Poe, famous American short-story writer and poet:—I have read Poe's "The Gold Bug."

—**pose** an attitude, bodily position:— The artist's model took another pose for her employer.

pole (rhymes with stole) 1. a long, narrow rounded stick used for displaying a flag, supporting a clothes-line, etc.:—Our school flag hangs from a tall white pole. 2. the extreme northern or southern point of the world: —Perry discovered the North Pole. 3. (Cap.) a native of Poland. 4. the positive or negative end of an electric circuit.

—**poll** secure the opinions or votes of:— A New York newspaper will poll the citizens of New York State on their choice for the next Governor of the State.

***poor** (rhymes with door) 1. opposite of rich, destitute:—Christ taught that the more fortunate should give to the poor. 2. not good or satisfactory: —We had a very poor steak at that restaurant. 3. unfortunate, pitiable: —The poor child suffered from a bad burn.

—**pore** 1. one of many small openings in the skin:—Sweat exudes through our pores. 2. read or examine minutely:—The scholar will pore over his manuscript until late in the evening.

—**pour** discharge or empty liquor from a vessel into another vessel or dish: —Please pour me another glassful of iced tea from the pitcher.

pore see poor

pose see Poe's

pour see poor

praise (rhymes with raise) 1. glorify God:—At church we sang hymns of praise. 2. compliment:—The teacher praised John for his excellent work in class.

—prays third person singular of pray, offer up prayers to God:—Every Sunday Tom prays in church.

—preys third person singular of prey, hunt down, victimize:—The fox preys on the rabbit.

pray (rhymes with say) 1. commune with God:—During the mass the priest prays. 2. beg:—I pray that you will be careful while driving on the highway.

—prey 1. victim:—The sheep is the wolf's prey. 2. victimize:—Thieves prey on their unsuspecting victims and steal from them.

prays see praise

presence (rhymes with peasants) in the company of, opposite of absence:—I will repeat the story in his presence.

—*presents gifts:—We exchange presents at Christmas.

prey see pray

preys see praise

pride (rhymes with lied, slide) a feeling of personal satisfaction:—Mr. Allen took great pride in his son's high standing in his school.

—pried past tense of pry. 1. force off a bottle cap, etc. with a lever:—With a knife I pried off the cover of the jelly jar. 2. intrude or snoop into another's affairs:—That employee was dismissed for having pried into his superior's correspondence.

pries (rhymes with tries) third person singular of pry, see pried above:—His wife never pries into his affairs.

—prize an award:—Jim received first prize in the athletic competition.

prince (rhymes with since) son of a king:—The Prince of Wales is the heir to the British throne.

—*prints (rhymes with tints) a drawing, a fabric, etc. printed on a printing press:—Martha is wearing a red print dress.

principal (rhymes with invincible) chief:—The head of a high school is usually called a principal. The principal reason he went south was to escape the cold northern winters.

—principle an ethical or physical law:—That employer pensions off his retiring employees as a matter of principle. The physics teacher explained to his class the principle of the steam engine.

prints see prince

prize see pries

profit (rhymes with doff it) a gain or receipt from a business transaction or other gain:—The retailer sold sixty-dollar dresses for ninety dollars and made a fifty percent profit. We studied Latin with much profit to our minds.

—prophet one who foretells the future:—Isaiah was a Biblical prophet.

pros (rhymes with goes) 1. plural of pro, a point in favor of, opposite of con:—We discussed the pros and cons of world federation. 2. plural of pro, a professional as compared to an amateur:—Amateur sports stars are not supposed to play with pros for money.

—prose written material or literary composition not in poetic or metrical form:—Many of Shakespeare's plays are in both prose and verse.

psalter (rhymes with Walter) the prayer book:—The priest read to his congregation out of a psalter.

—salter one who salts food etc., or a dish that holds salt:—The Cloisters Museum has a collection of Renaissance silver salters.

pshaw (rhymes with saw, raw) an exclamation expressing annoyance or disgust:—Oh pshaw! I had expected you home for dinner tonight, and now you say you have to work late.

—Shaw a surname.
purl see pearl
pursy see Percy
purveyed see pervade

Q

Q (rhymes with who, you) 17th letter of the alphabet. See **cue**
quarts (rhymes with sorts) plural of **quart**, a liquid measure equal to two pints:—I bought two quarts of milk in containers.
—**quartz** a translucent or transparent mineral used in optical work, often a clear white or rose color:—We have a dish made of rose quartz.
queue see **cue**
quire see **choir**

R

R see **are**
rain (rhymes with gain) 1. waterdrops falling from the clouds:—A shower is a heavy rain. 2. anything that falls in quantity:—The spectators, angered at the umpire's decision, rained pop bottles on him.
—**reign** rule as king or queen, etc.:— Queen Elizabeth reigns in Great Britain.
—**rein** one of the two leather lines connected to the horse's head and mouth, the other end held by the driver or rider of the horse:—Wishing to stop the carriage, the driver pulled on both reins.
raise (rhymes with pays) 1. lift, elevate:—When students raise their hands, they want to recite. 2. an increase in salary:—Mary's firm gave her a raise last month. 3. grow or produce food:—Farmer White raises turnips and pigs.
—**rays** plural of **ray**, a beam of light:— The early rays of the sun awoke me.
—**raze** tear down, demolish:—The city plans to raze the obsolete buildings in the slums in order to build new housing projects.
raiser (rhymes with praiser) one who

lifts or grows something:—Farmer Green is a raiser of beef cattle.
—**razor** a sharp-bladed cutting instrument for shaving off a man's beard: —John uses a safety razor.
rancor (rhymes with banker) enmity, resentment:—Insulted by his enemy, the injured man, full of rancor, planned revenge.
—**ranker** comparative of **rank** 1. offensive:—Murder is a ranker crime than theft. 2. of excessive growth:—The grass grows ranker in a swamp than on a lawn.
rap (rhymes with cap) knock, tap, or strike lightly with the knuckles so as to attract attention or to punish: —The postman with a special-delivery package began to rap on our door.
—**wrap** an overcovering for arms and shoulders, like a shawl:—She wore a mink wrap over her party dress.
rapt (rhymes with tapped) intensely absorbed, carried away from reality: —She listened to the violin sonata with a rapt expression on her face.
—**wrapped** past tense of **wrap**, cover or enclose with paper etc.:—The clerk wrapped the merchandise I had just purchased.
ray (rhymes with day) a narrow beam or shaft of light:—An early ray of the sun awakened me.
—**re²** the second note in the musical solfège scale:—Re comes after do.
rays see **raise**
raze see **raise**
razor see **raiser**
re² see **ray**
read¹ (rhymes with need) 1. peruse a book, magazine or newspaper, letter, etc. silently:—I can read French easily. 2. speak aloud the words of a book:—When we were too young to read, Mother would read us fairy stories.
—**reed** a stalk of tall grass or material woven from this grass, a cane:—Our neighbors have reed furniture on their sun-porch.

read² (rhymes with bed) past tense of read¹:—When we were children, our nurse often read to us.

—**red** the bright primary color:—Blood is red and roses are red.

real (rhymes with wheel, deal) actual, genuine:—This pocketbook is made of real leather.

—**reel** 1. a revolving cylinder around which rope, twine, etc. is wound:—Most fishermen have a reel on their pole. 2. stagger, feel dizzy:—After the thief hit him, the policeman began to reel from the blow.

reck (rhymes with neck) heed, count the cost of:—Little did the hero reck the danger involved in rescuing the drowning man.

—**wreck** something smashed or otherwise made inoperable:—By driving into a tree, the sleepy driver made a wreck of his car.

recover (rhymes with tea lover) 1. get well after an illness:—It took Justine three weeks to recover from the flu. 2. regain possession of property lost, stolen, etc:—The police managed to recover all of the stolen jewelry except two rings.

—**re-cover** cover anew:—We had our shabby upholstered furniture re-covered.

red see **read²**

reed see **read¹**

reek (rhymes with seek) smell very strongly and unpleasantly of:—After a family party the living-room always reeks of cigar smoke.

—**wreak** bring upon, inflict:—The wronged soldier planned to wreak vengeance on his enemy.

reel see **real**

reign see **rain**

rein see **rain**

residence (rhymes with hesitance) the place where one lives, a house or an apartment, etc:—My residence is in Manhattan.

—*****residents** plural of **resident**, a person living in a certain locality:—All the residents of New York have access to Central Park.

rest (rhymes with best) 1. the remainder, what is left over:—Don grabbed two suitcases, and his wife picked up the rest of the luggage. 2. relax, repose:—Mother rests every day after lunch. 3. lie on, be supported by:—The book rests on the table.

—**wrest** twist, snatch from by twisting:—The policeman managed to wrest the pistol from the thief.

retch (rhymes with fetch) vomit, try to throw up the contents of one's stomach:—The sight of the murdered man made the young boy retch.

—**wretch** a very unfortunate person who deserves to be pitied, or an evil person:—That wretch was hanged for the murder of his wife.

review (rhymes with redo) 1. a published criticism of a book, play, concert, etc.:—I like to read book reviews. 2. prepare for exams by going over material previously studied:—I stayed up all night to review for my final exams.

—**revue** a theatrical production featuring humorous or satirical skits, sketches, and songs.:—The Little Show was a famous revue.

rhyme (rhymes with time) two words rhyme when they match in vowel sounds and final consonant sounds:—"Cat" rhymes with "rat" and "sat."

—**rime** the white frost that forms on a cold windowpane:—We used to scratch drawings on the window rime.

rigger (rhymes with trigger) one who raises or lowers heavy loads:—We had to hire a rigger to hoist our piano into the apartment.

—**rigor** 1. stiffness:—A short time after death, rigor sets in the body. 2. harshness, severity:—We suffered the rigor of a very cold winter.

right (rhymes with bite) 1. opposite of left:—I write with my right hand. 2. ethically correct:—To ask forgiveness of the person that you have wronged is the right thing to do. 3. a legal privilege:—Every American citizen has certain constitutional rights.

—**rite** a religious or fraternal ceremony: Last rites were administered to the dying man by the priest.

—**wright** a maker or a worker such as a shipwright, millwright, playwright, etc.

—**write** use pen and pencil, put down words on paper, typewrite, etc.: —Mary writes with her left hand.

rigor see **rigger**

rime see **rhyme**

ring (rhymes with sing) 1. a circular piece of metal with a center opening, a band:—Susan wears both an engagement ring and a wedding ring. 2. the sound made by a bell:—The ring of our telephone is too loud. 3. a gang:—The police broke up a large gambling ring. 4. a boxing arena:—The two boxers stood inside the ring.

—**wring** 1. press or twist water out of a soaking wet cloth:—After she had washed her cotton dress, Esther had to wring it out. 2. twist one's hands in worry or sorrow:—Worry about having to have an operation made Mary wring her hands.

rise (rhymes with size) 1. be elevated or raised:—Prices will rise this fall. 2. stand or get up:—The teacher told her pupils to rise and salute the flag. 3. begin, start up:—Trouble will always rise in city slums.

—**ryes** plural of rye, a type of grain or the whiskey made from it:—I drank two ryes at the bar.

rite see **right**

road (rhymes with code) a street, highway, or path for vehicles:—Our house stands near a busy road.

—**rode** past tense of ride, journey on horseback, in a car, train, etc.: We rode through Holland on a de luxe bus.

—**rowed** past tense of row[1], scull or propel a boat by means of oars:— John rowed on the college crew.

roam (rhymes with home) wander or travel about rather aimlessly:—On his vacation Carl will roam through the various cities of Europe.

—**Rome** the capital city of Italy.

roar (rhymes with core) 1. the deep, thunderous sound that a lion, thunder, or an explosion makes:—The lion's roar made us jump.

—**rower** one who rows or propels a boat with oars:—After the race, the rower looked tired.

rode see **road**

roe (rhymes with go) the eggs of a fish: —At dinner we were served shad roe.

—**row**[1] 1. a line of seats in a theatre, etc.:—At the play we sat in the third row. 2. use oars to propel a boat:— I learned to row at camp. 3. a line of objects:—The small lad placed his toy soldiers all in a row.

role (rhymes with pole, stole) the playing part taken by an actor:— John Barrymore's famous role was Hamlet.

—**roll** 1. a small, usually circular, baked piece of bread, a bun:—We had rolls and coffee for breakfast. 2. turn over and over rapidly:—We watched the ball roll across the lawn. 3. an attendance list:—The teacher called the roll after our class started.

Rome see **roam**

rood (rhymes with food) the cross of Christ:—He swore upon the rood to be a good knight.

—**rude** 1. impolite, discourteous:—As the young girl walked by, the boys made rude remarks about her. 2. unpolished, rough:—He lived in a rude house made of logs.

—**rued** past tense of **rue**, regret, be sorry for:—We rued the day that we ever agreed to serve lunch to forty boy scouts.

roomer (rhymes with tumor) one who rents a room to live in:—Mrs. Slade takes in roomers.

—**rumor** gossip, hearsay, unconfirmed reports:—There is a rumor that the Secretary of Labor will resign.

root (rhymes with boot) 1. source, foundation:—Trade with China was root of that family's wealth. 2. a part of the plant that grows underground:—The roots of that large tree are deep in the soil.

—**route** a way, path:—We took the shorter route to the shore.

rose (rhymes with goes) 1. a kind of flower:—Roses grow on rose bushes. 2. past tense of **rise**, be elevated:—Prices of wheat rose on the commodity market.

—**rows**¹ 1. plural of **row**, a line of objects:—We like to sit in the first row.

rote (rhymes with coat) repeating, repetition:—The child learned his alphabet by rote.

—**wrote** past tense of **write**:—I wrote a letter to my sister yesterday.

rough (rhymes with tough, stuff) 1. not smooth:—Sandpaper has a rough surface. 2. ungentle:—Boys like to play rough games like football. 3. unfinished, preliminary:—I made a rough sketch of my proposed house for the guidance of the architect.

—**ruff** a starched circular neckpiece or collar worn in the seventeenth century:—Van Dyck painted many portraits of men wearing ruffs.

rouse (rhymes with cows) awaken, alert, stir up a person:—The danger from the Indians would rouse all the colonists.

—**rows**² (rhymes with cows) plural of **row**², a noisy quarrel:—Mr. Hamilton constantly had rows with his wife.

route see **root**

row¹ see **roe**

rowed see **road**

rower see **roar**

rows¹ see **rose**

rows² see **rouse**

rude see **rood**

rued see **rood**

rues (rhymes with choose) third person singular of **rue**, regret:—He rues the day he turned down that job.

—**ruse** a stratagem, clever plan:—The Greeks obtained entrance to Troy by the ruse of the wooden Trojan Horse.

ruff see **rough**

rumor see **roomer**

rung (rhymes with sung) 1. past participle of **ring**, sound a bell:—I have rung that bell six times already without getting any service. 2. a horizontal step on a ladder:—That ladder has twelve rungs.

—**wrung** past participle of **wring**, twist:—After she had washed the sheet, and wrung out all the water, she took it outside and hung it on the line to dry.

ruse see **rues**

rye (rhymes with try) 1. a particular variety of grain or cereal or a whisky made from this grain:—That field is sowed with rye. I drank two ryes before dinner. 2. rye bread:—I'll have a ham on rye. See a rye—awry.

—**wry** distorted, twisted:—He made a wry face after he drank the bitter medicine.

ryes see **rise**

S

sac (rhymes with back) a skin membrane holding a liquid:—A blister is a sac.

—**sack** a bag made of rough cloth such as a potato sack:—We bought a sack of onions.

—**sacque** a quilted robe for a woman or baby:—Mother is sewing a sacque for her baby grandson.

sail (rhymes with fail) 1. a heavy triangular piece of coarse cloth or canvas, attached to an upright mast, which propels a ship in the wind:—That small ship has only one sail. 2. a trip in a boat:—We took a sail up the Hudson last week.

—sale 1. transfer of ownership from seller to buyer:—After the clerk receives money from a customer, she rings up the amount of the sale. 2. a time of selling goods at reduced prices:—Tomorrow they are having sale at Macy's on shirts.

salter see psalter

saver (rhymes with braver) one who saves or preserves, or that which saves:—Savers put their money in savings banks. That increase in pay was a life-saver.

—savor taste, smell:—That roast beef has a delightful savor.

scene (rhymes with green) 1. prospect, view:—Constable painted many scenes of rural life. 2. section or division of a play:—The play of "Hamlet" opens with a scene on the battlements. 3. a fuss or altercation; a noisy complaint in public:—When the waitress brought the customer a burned steak, the latter made a scene.

—seen past participle of see:—I have seen that movie more than once.

scent see cent

scents see cense

scull (rhymes with dull) propel a boat with a single oar or double oars:—We watched the rower scull the boat up the Charles River.

—skull the bony headpiece of man and other animals that encloses the brain:—Tom fractured his skull in an automobile accident.

sea see C

sealing see ceiling

seam (rhymes with dream) 1. the edges where two pieces of cloth sewn together meet:—Mother sews a very fine seam. 2. a vein of coal or other mineral:—The miners are cutting a newly discovered seam of coal.

—seem appear:—Jack seems to be a nice chap. My cold doesn't seem to be getting any better.

sear (rhymes with near) scorch or burn the outside of a piece of meat or one's flesh:—The cook sears the roast before cooking it.

—seer an oracle, a foreteller of events:—Tiresias was a famous Greek seer.

—sere old and withered:—Leaves brown and sere were blown about by the icy wind.

seas see C's

see see C

seed see cede

seem see seam

seen see scene

seer see sear

seize see C's

sell see cell

seller see cellar

sense see cense

sent see cent

sere see sear

serf (rhymes with turf) a slave, one bound to serve a master or owner of land on which he works:—The Russian Revolution freed many a serf.

—surf the waves of the sea as they break and dash onto the beach:—We like to swim and fish in the surf.

serge (rhymes with merge, purge) a diagonally ribbed woolen suiting or cloth:—I have a blue serge suit.

—surge rise up, swell quickly and fall just as ocean waves do:—The surge of the waves bounced our small boat up and down. Watch that excited crowd surge forward to see the President.

serial see cereal

series see Ceres

sew (rhymes with go) join two pieces of cloth with a needle and thread or with a sewing machine, attach buttons:—Mother promised to sew new buttons on my shirt.

—**so** 1. therefore:—It rained, so we stayed home. 2. very:—My friend is so kind and thoughtful. 3. as . . . as I am:—I don't like to be so insistent, but I need the money you owe me.

—**sow¹** 1. plant seeds or ideas:—The farmer sows his field with wheat. 2. Enemies of the nation try to sow discontent among the loyal citizens.

sewer² (rhymes with goer) one who sews, uses needle and thread:—Edith is a sewer on women's dresses.

—**sower** one who sows or scatters seeds into the ground:—Christ taught the parable of the sower.

shanty see **chanty**

Shaw see **pshaw**

shear (rhymes with fear) cut with a shears, knife, or other sharp instrument:—That machine is designed to shear off the bark from the logs.

—**sheer** 1. very transparent:—Mary likes to wear sheer silk stockings. 2. pure, unalloyed:—To hear that opera star sing was sheer pleasure. 3. twist or turn:—We watched the pilot of the ship sheer off from the rocks just in time to avoid a catastrophe.

sheik see **chic**

shoe (rhymes with true) 1. footgear or boots worn over socks or stockings:—Connie bought a new pair of high-heeled shoes last Saturday. 2. outside part of an automobile tire:—I need a new shoe and a new inner tube for my left front wheel. 3. put metal horseshoes on a horse:—Blacksmiths shoe horses.

—**shoo** push out, drive out:—The housekeeper will shoo the cat out of the living-room.

shone (rhymes with bone) past tense of **shine**, reflect light:—The moon shone brilliantly last night.

—**shown** past participle of **show**, reveal, display, demonstrate:—Although the salesman had shown us how to operate the sewing machine, we had some trouble making it go. We were shown some exclusive dresses from Paris.

shoo see **shoe**

shoot see **chute**

shown see **shone**

sic (rhymes with Dick, thick) set or try to set a dog on another person:—The houseowner threatened to sic his large dog on the abusive beggar.

—**sick** ill, in bad health:—Tom is at home sick and cannot attend the meeting.

side (rhymes with ride) 1. a wall or partition:—The paint is worn off the northern side of that house. 2. in a direction or place opposite to another direction or place:—We live on the east side of the river.

—**sighed** past tense of **sigh**, exhale slowly with a sign of regret, boredom, or relief:—Henry sighed when he thought of the girl he might have married and didn't. John sighed when he remembered all the homework he had to do.

sider see **cider**

sighed see **side**

sighs (rhymes with buys) third person singular of **sigh**, exhale the breath slowly to indicate sorrow, regret, etc.:—When John thinks of all the money he lost on gambling, he sighs.

—**size** indicating the dimensions of a surface or solid:—Allan wears a size 16 shirt. What is the size of their house?

sight see **cite**

sign (rhymes with wine) 1. a board or placard on which lettering is placed warning, announcing, giving directions, etc.:—The sign at the side of the road read: Boston 45 miles. 2. affix one's signature to a document:—The buyer won't sign the contract as he had agreed to. 3. indication, appearance:—There was no sign of fever in the patient.

—**sine** a mathematical concept used in trigonometry.

site *see* **cite**
size *see* **sighs**
skull *see* **scull**
slay (rhymes with day) kill, murder:—
The enraged husband vowed to slay
his unfaithful wife.
—sleigh a large cart, wagon, or carriage
on runners used for the transportation of people or goods over ice and
snow:—During the last snowfall our
class all went for a sleigh-ride.
sleight (rhymes with bright) skill:—The
magician astonished us with his
sleight-of-hand tricks.
—slight 1. little, small:—Mr. Jones is
tall and heavy, but his wife is slight.
There will be a slight delay while
the bus is having its tire changed.
2. neglect:—When I invited Tom to
dinner I didn't mean to slight his
sister by not asking her too.
so *see* **sew**
soar (rhymes with core) rise rapidly upwards in the air:—Our plane will
quickly soar to 15,000 feet.
—sore 1. painful:—I have a very sore
back from sunburn. 2. angry (colloq.):
—Mary ran up a large bill at the
department store and this made her
husband sore.
soared (rhymes with board) past tense
of soar, rise rapidly:—Prices have
soared this past year.
—sword a long wide steel weapon with
a sharp blade:—In olden days a
nobleman wore a sword at his side.
sol (rhymes with stole, mole) the fifth
note of the musical scale:—Do, re,
mi, fa, sol are the first five notes of
the solfège scale.
—sole 1. the bottom of a shoe except
for the heel:—I wear rubber soles.
2. only:—Yesterday I was the sole
passenger on the bus.
—soul the non-physical part of a man
declared to be immortal:—Man's soul
lives after him.
sold (rhymes with cold) past tense of
sell, exchange goods or services for
money:—Meats and vegetables were
sold at that store.

—soled past tense of sole, affix new
soles on worn shoes:—I had my shoes
rubber soled.
sole *see* **sol**
some (rhymes with come) 1. pronoun
meaning part but not all:—Some of
my students come from South America. 2. an indefinite degree of:—I
have some trouble with my car.
—sum 1. total:—The sum of 3 and 2 is
5. 2. amount:—Ten dollars is quite
a sum to pay for a necktie.
son (rhymes with gun) a male child
often called "son" by his parents:—
The Browns have two daughters and
one son. It's time for bed, Son.
—sun the source of our terrestrial light
and heat:—Don't stay too long in the
sun and get sunburned.
sore *see* **soar**
soul *see* **sol**
sow¹ *see* **sew**
sower *see* **sewer²**
staid (rhymes with paid) of a conserva-
tive, serious makeup:—My grandmother was very staid in her ways.
—stayed past tense of stay, remain:—I
left the party early, but Joan stayed.
stair (rhymes with care) one of a series
of steps leading from one storey to
another, which are called stairs:—
Each stair in that house is covered
with a rubber foot-tread.
—stare look intently at something or
someone:—The country dweller likes
to come to the city and stare at the
sights.
stake (rhymes with bake) 1. a short
stick sharpened at one end used to
hold down a tent, etc.:—We erected
a tent and then drove stakes into
the ground to hold the guy ropes.
2. a wager or an investment:—How
much is your partner's stake in your
dry-cleaning business?
—steak a slice of beef broiled or fried:
—Most Americans enjoy a good piece
of steak.
stare *see* **stair**
stationary (rhymes with ration Harry)
unmoving, fixed, rooted:—Most

homes except trailers are stationary.

—**stationery** writing paper, envelopes, etc.:—I bought some stationery with my name and address printed on it.

stayed see **staid**

steak see **stake**

steal (rhymes with feel) unlawfully take property of another without his consent:—John saw Max steal his roommate's watch.

—**steel** a metal made from iron:—My kitchen knives are made of steel.

step (rhymes with pep) 1. walk:—We had to step lively to avoid getting drenched in the rain. 2. a stair:—There are three steps up to our front door.

—**steppe** a broad flat piece of land in Russia:—Deep snow covered the steppe in winter.

stile (rhymes with tile) steps on the opposite sides of a fence for the convenience of persons crossing a field:—We climbed up the stile in order to get into the next field.

—**style** way, manner, fashion:—I like that author's style of writing. Her dress is in the very latest style.

storey (rhymes with lorry, hoary) one of the floor levels of a building:—Our house is three storeys high. They live on the fourth storey which is three flights up.

—**story** 1. a narrative, tale:—Every Sunday Mother used to tell us a story from the Bible. 2. a lie, untruth:—Mother punished Joan for telling stories about how mean I had been to her.

straight (rhymes with late) 1. not crooked, uncurved:—A straight line is the shortest distance between two points. 2. correct:—Did you get the message straight? 3. undiluted:—He drinks his whisky straight.

—**strait** a narrow passage of water connecting two larger bodies of water:—The Dardanelles is the name of a strait.

straightened past tense of straighten, make something crooked straight:—I straightened out a piece of bent wire.

—**straitened** poor, poverty-stricken:—Ever since he lost his job, his wife and children have been in very straitened circumstances.

strait see **straight**

straitened see **straightened**

style see **stile**

succor (rhymes with trucker) aid, assist, shield from harm:—Christ sought to succor men from evil.

—**sucker** (slang.) a dupe, easy-mark:—That sucker just paid fifty dollars for a watch not worth five.

suede (rhymes with fade) leather that has been rubbed so that it has the texture of cloth:—She was wearing a suede jacket.

—**swayed** past tense of sway 1. swing back and forth:—The small branches of the tree swayed in the wind. 2. influence:—The clever politician swayed his audience and won many votes.

suite (rhymes with heat) 1. a group of two or more adjoining rooms:—The President took a large suite of rooms at his hotel in order to accommodate his large staff. 2. a set of matching pieces of furniture:—We have just bought a new bedroom suite.

—**sweet** 1. sugary, not sour:—I don't like to have my coffee too sweet, so I use only a half a lump of sugar. 2. fresh:—Unsalted butter is sweet. 3. affectionate:—He is very sweet to his mother.

sum see **some**

sun see **son**

sundae (rhymes with Monday) a dish of ice-cream with a sweet syrupy topping:—I stopped in the drugstore and ate a chocolate sundae.

—**Sunday** the first day of the week:—Most people have a day off on Sunday.

surf see **serf**

surge see **serge**

swayed see **suede**

sweet see **suite**
sword see **soared**
symbol see **cymbal**

T

T (rhymes with she) the 20th letter of the alphabet:—There are two t's in "battle."

—**te** seventh note in the musical solfège scale.

—**tea** 1. the common beverage made of hot water and tea leaves:—I had a cup of tea and a sandwich for lunch. 2. an afternoon party or reception where tea and/or cocktails are served:—Fifty attended the Brown's tea.

—**tee** in golf, the starting point for playing each particular hole:—Four of us gathered at the tee of the first hole and started to play.

tacked (rhymes with backed) fasten together with a small nail:—We tacked the calendar to the wall.

—**tact** the quality of being less than frank, careful of others' feelings, skillful in managing difficult situations:—A hostess needs great tact in dealing with the varying opinions and prejudices of her guests.

tacks (rhymes with sacks) plural of tack, a small large-headed metal nail:—I need another box of tacks to finish tacking down the stair carpet.

—**tax** 1. the governmental levy on property, income, etc.:—Most Americans have to pay an income tax. 2. strain, burden, sap:—Overtime work at the office will tax his strength.

tact see **tacked**

tail (rhymes with fail) 1. the familiar appendage of a dog, cat, etc.:—The friendly dog wagged his tail when I patted his head. 2. that side of a coin opposite the figure of a head:—Heads I win, tails you lose. (said jokingly when tossing a coin)

—**tale** a story, narrative:—Andersen and Grimm wrote fairy tales.

tare (rhymes with care) a worthless weed:—The wheat was in danger of being choked by tares.

—**tear**[2] rip apart usually into two or more pieces:—He began to tear his manuscript into many pieces. Little boys usually tear their trousers when they try to climb trees.

taught (rhymes with bought) past tense of **teach**, instruct:—When we were very young, Mother taught us how to read.

—**taut** drawn or pulled tight, said of a straightened rope, opposite of loose or slack:—The violinist's strings were very taut.

tax see **tacks**

tea see **T**

team (rhymes with theme, steam) 1. an organized group, especially in sports:—There are eleven players on a football team. 2. two, a pair:—That farmer has a good team of horses.

—**teem** be full of:—That mountain stream is said to teem with fish.

tear[1] (rhymes with dear) natural drop of water from the eye-ducts:—A tear ran down Mary's cheek when she was forbidden to go to the movies.

—**tier**[1] layers, storeys, or levels:—We sat in the upper tier of seats in the stadium. That wedding cake has five tiers.

tear[2] see **tare**

teas (rhymes with fees) plural of tea, the popular beverage made of hot water and tea leaves:—Our grocer carries several brands of teas.

—**tease** 1. make fun of another so as to provoke an outburst:—Mary's older brother likes to tease her about her boy-friend's bashfulness. 2. beg for:—Stop teasing for an ice-cream cone. It's too near dinner time.

—**tees** plural of tee, a place where a hole of golf starts:—The first and second tees of that course are on lower ground.

—**T's** plural of **T**

tee see **T**

tees see **tease**

teem see **team**

tense (rhymes with dense) 1. one of the six time categories of English verbs:—"I am" is in the present tense. 2. not relaxed, tightened muscularly:—Worry made him very tense.

—***tents** (rhymes with dents) plural of **tent**, a portable canvas shelter supported by poles and ropes:—Many soldiers live in tents.

their (rhymes with care) possessive of **they**:—Mr. and Mrs. Smith invited us to their home for dinner.

—**there** opposite of **here**:—That letter isn't in my pocket; it's over there on the table.

—**they're** contraction of **they are**:—Where are John and Mary? They're late.

threw (rhymes with few) past tense of **throw**, hurl:—The pitcher threw the ball to the catcher.

—**through** 1. finished. I am through with this book and will return it to the library. 2. passing from one side to the other:—The boy on the inside threw the ball outside through the open window. 3. by means of:—Through his senatorial father, John was able to meet the President.

throe (rhymes with show) a mental or physical pain, often in the plural:—Most mothers have experienced the throes of childbirth.

—**throw** toss or hurl:—Throw me a cigarette, will you?

throne (rhymes with bone) 1. the raised seat of a king:—After the king ascended the throne, his courtiers took their seats. 2. also the king or his power:—Edward VIII of England renounced his throne. Those socialistic policies of Parliament will never be approved of by the throne.

—**thrown** past participle of **throw**, toss or hurl to the ground:—That football player was thrown on the 40-yard line.

through see **threw**

throw see **throe**

thrown see **throne**

tic (rhymes with sick) an involuntary twitching of facial muscles:—The doctors have been unable to cure Marcia's tic.

—**tick** the regular sound a watch or clock makes:—The tick of my wrist watch is barely audible.

tide (rhymes with ride) 1. the hourly variations in the distance the ocean runs inshore or away from the shore:—We prefer to go swimming at high tide. 2. a time or season:—Christmastide is a joyous season.

—**tied** past tense of **tie**, fasten:—Mother tied on her apron and washed the dishes.

tier[1] see **tear**[1]

tier[2] (rhymes with buyer) one who ties or fastens:—That boy scout won a medal as a tier of knots.

—**tire**:—1. cause tiredness or exhaustion:—That long climb up the mountain will tire her. 2. a circular rubber casing for the wheels of an automobile or other vehicle:—My left front wheel needs a new tire.

to (rhymes with who) 1. preposition indicating direction towards:—I am going to Boston. 2. used in the infinitive form:—I like to dance. 3. in order to:—I closed the window to keep out the cold wind.

—**too** 1. also:—I am studying French and John is too. 2. excessively:—It's too noisy in here; I can't hear myself think. That fur coat costs too much.

—**two** the numeral between one and three:—I have two eyes and two ears.

toad (rhymes with code) a small hopping animal like a frog:—There are small toads in our garden.

—**toed** past tense of **toe**, stand upon one's toes:—Before the race each contestant toed the starting line.

—**towed** past tense of **tow**, pull or drag by a rope or chain:—Small tugs always towed the large ocean liners into their docks.

toe (rhymes with go) one of the fingers of the foot:—On each foot I have four small toes and one big toe.

—**tow** 1. pull or haul a ship or car, etc.:—Our car broke down and a wrecker came to tow us. 2. very light-colored hair:—That girl is a tow-head.

toed see **toad**

told (rhymes with sold) past tense of tell, inform:—He told me an untrue story.

—**tolled** past tense of toll, ring a large bell slowly and repeatedly:—The church bell tolled for the funeral.

ton (rhymes with run) 2,000 pounds in weight:—Coal is sold by the ton.

—**tun** a large case or vat for holding liquids, especially wine:—The king always kept a tun or two of sherry in his cellar.

too see **to, two**

tool (rhymes with school, rule) an instrument or implement for doing work:—A screwdriver is a handy tool.

—**tulle** a gauzy light-weight silk or other fabric:—Her party dress was made of pink tulle.

tow see **toe**

towed see **toad**

tracked (rhymes with fact) past tense of track, make or follow footprints:—The child tracked a lot of mud into the house. The hunters tracked the bear across the snow.

—**tract** 1. a religious pamphlet.—On the street corner the members of a religious sect were handing out tracts to all comers. 2. a section of land:—William Penn secured a large tract of land in America.

tri (rhymes with cry) prefix meaning three:—We flew in a tri-motored airplane.

—**try** 1. attempt:—I'll try to put up the window, but yesterday it stuck fast. 2. test:—Let's try Carl on a new job and see how well he does. 3. strain, upset:—James's stupidity tries his teacher's patience. 4. give a legal trial to:—That court will try the prisoner for robbery.

troop (rhymes with soup) an organized group of soldiers, boy scouts, etc.:—Because of the strike riots, the Governor called out the state troops.

—**troupe** a group or company of organized theatrical folk:—The special train brought a troupe of circus entertainers to town.

trussed (rhymes with must) past tense of truss, tie up:—The robber trussed the householder in rope and stole some valuable jewels.

—**trust** 1. have confidence in:—I trust my wife absolutely. 2. extend credit to:—I haven't any money with me. Will you trust me for these groceries until tomorrow?

try see **tri**

T's see **tease**

tucks (rhymes with ducks) 1. plural of tuck, a pleat or fold:—Mother sewed tucks into her curtains. 2. press into a pocket:—When he received his pay, he tucked it into his pocket.

—**tux** short for **tuxedo**, a dinner-jacket worn by men on formal occasions:—Jim wore a tux for the formal college dance.

tulle see **tool**

tun see **ton**

tux see **tucks**

'twill (rhymes with bill) contraction for it will:—'Twill be eleven o'clock in a few minutes.

—**twill** a diagonally woven cloth or fabric:—Her coat is made of twill fabric.

two see **to**

U

U see **ewe**

urn see **earn**

V

vain (rhymes with train) 1. overly and offensively proud of one's looks, ability, clothes, etc.:—The peacock is a vain bird. 2. useless, ineffectual:—The rescuer made a vain effort to save the drowning man.

—**vane** 1. a weather vane that turns on its axis with the wind, showing the various directions of the wind:—There is a vane on the top of our house. 2. one of a series of shutters:—I opened one of the vanes on my air conditioner.

—**vein** 1. a blood vessel returning impure blood to the heart and lungs:—The nurse injected medicine into the patient's vein. 2. a streak or layer of ore in a rock or mine wall:—Recently a new vein of coal was discovered in an abandoned mine. 3. disposition, way, manner:—Ralph spoke in a humorous vein.

vale (rhymes with nail) a valley:—We lived in a small vale beside a high mountain.

—**veil** 1. a finely meshed or netted cloth worn completely or partially over a woman's face to disguise or enhance her looks:—Mrs. Long wore a half veil over her forehead and eyes. 2. screen, hide:—Venetian blinds veil the living-room furniture and rugs from the sun.

vane see **vain**

veil see **vale**

vein see **vain**

vial (rhymes with dial) a small tube or glass bottle for drugs, medicines, etc.:—The druggist sold me a vial of sleeping tablets.

—**vile** 1. hateful, wicked, most offensive:—To murder his host was a vile deed. There was a vile odor in the room from burning wool. 2. lowest in the social scale:—That famous medieval poet was of vile birth.

W

WACS (rhymes with backs) the U.S. Women's Auxiliary Corps of the U.S. Army:—During the last war many young women served in the WACS and the WAVES.

—**wax** 1. the solid yellow part of honey, also similar material deposited in the ear canals:—I had the doctor remove the excess wax in my ears. 2. grows:—The young baby began to wax strong and fat.

wade (rhymes with fade) walk with hindrance through water or other slowly yielding substance:—The small children love to wade in the shallow brook. It took me three days to wade through that long novel.

—**weighed** past tense of weigh 1. determine the heaviness of:—The grocer weighed the bananas before mentioning the price. Before his illness, Tom weighed 175 pounds. 2. burden, oppress:—Shortage of money weighed on her mind.

wail (rhymes with fail) complain, cry out in a loud voice:—That sick baby will wail all day.

—**wale** a cloth woven with ridges:—Mary wore a pinwale cotton skirt.

wain (rhymes with grain) a wagon:—Charles's Wain is a constellation.

—**wane** opposite of wax, decrease:—The moon waxes and wanes every month.

—**Wayne** a proper name.

waist (rhymes with haste) that part of the human body that one passes a belt around:—Around her waist she wore a red sash.

—**waste** 1. discarded useless material such as garbage, old paper, sewerage, etc.: That river is choked with waste from a nearby factory. 2. use needlessly so as to decrease the stock of, or uneconomically fail to use:—Have your water faucets fixed so that they don't waste water.

wait (rhymes with late) delay, linger, stay in one spot:—I can't wait for the bus any longer; I'm going to walk to work.

—**weight** 1. heaviness or the measure of heaviness:—In that reducing diet I lost a lot of weight. 2. a heavy metal measure:—Put a weight on those papers or they will blow away. 3. influence:—His father's advice carries great weight with John.

waive (rhymes with save) surrender, pass up:—The heir agreed to waive all rights in the property for $5,000.

—**wave** 1. back and forward motion of the hands, similar motion of a flag in the wind, etc.:—When Mother sailed for France, we waved goodbye to her from the pier. 2. the ocean surf:—The waves at the beach are pretty high today. I don't think I'll go in.

wale see **wail**

wane see **wain**

ward (rhymes with cord) 1. a person under 21, a minor placed under the protection of a legal guardian other than either of his parents:—George is a ward of his uncle. 2. a section of a hospital for groups of patients:—I saw Mrs. Little in the maternity ward. 3. a section of a city:—He votes in the Third Ward. 4. protect, keep off:—Vaccination will ward off disease.

—**warred** past tense of war, make war on or attack another nation:—Germany warred against Russia.

ware (rhymes with care) fabricated merchandise, especially hardware such as kitchenware, dishes, pots and pans, etc.:—The salesman showed us aluminum ware.

—**wear** 1. cover the body with hats, suits, dresses, etc.:—Be sure to wear warm clothing on your trip up north. 2. last or keep, said of clothing:—How well did that suit wear?

warred see **ward**

waste see **waist**

wave see **waive**

wax see **WACS**

way (rhymes with day) direction, manner, wish:—Are you walking my way? I don't like his way of criticising everybody. If he has his way, we'll all take a cut in salary.

—**weigh** 1. measure the number of pounds a person or object weighs:—That mother has to weigh her newborn baby every day. 2. consider, evaluate:—John will weigh the offer of a new job from every angle.

Wayne see **wane**

we (rhymes with tree) plural of the pronoun I:—John and I like music so much that we go to concerts regularly.

—**wee** very small, minute, tiny:—Please give me a wee bit more cream in my coffee.

weak (rhymes with Greek) feeble, not strong:—That patient is still very weak after his operation and has to stay in bed.

—**week** seven consecutive days from Sunday to Saturday or any part of it:—I'll phone you next week for sure. We spent two weeks at the beach.

weal (rhymes with feel) prosperity, good fortune:—He is faithful to his trust come weal or woe.

—**we'll** contraction of we will:—We'll be glad to have you call on us.

wear see **ware**

weave (rhymes with leave) 1. construct fabric or cloth by crisscrossing threads:—That girl can weave baskets out of wood splints. 2. stagger as a drunk does:—See that drunk weave all over the sidewalk.

—**we've** contraction of we have:—We've seen that movie twice.

we'd (rhymes with need) contraction of we had or we would:—If we'd studied harder, we'd have passed the course.

—**weed** pull up weeds (useless plants) growing around useful plants:—We have to weed our garden daily.

wee see **we**

weed see **we'd**

week see **weak**

weigh see **way**

weighed see **wade**

weight see **wait**

weld (rhymes with spelled) fasten, join, or fuse two pieces of metal by partially melting or softening their ends:—I broke my car axle and had to have the mechanic weld it.

—welled past tense of well, spring to the surface:—Her feelings being hurt, tears welled up in her eyes.

we'll see weal

welled see weld

we've see weave

whole see hole

wholly see holy

whore see hoar

who's (rhymes with stews, blues) contraction of who is:—I wonder who's coming to the party.

—whose relative possessive pronoun:— I know whose car Jack is driving.

wise (rhymes with cries) very sage and intelligent:—The infant Jesus was visited by the three wise men.

—Y's plural of Y, the 25th. letter of the alphabet:—There are two y's in "yeasty."

won see one

wood (rhymes with stood) material of the tree such as the trunk and branches, or lumber:—That house is made entirely of wood.

—would 1. past tense of will, verb expressing future time:—My wife told me that George would call me. 2. used at the conclusion of a present unreal condition:—If I knew that girl, I would speak to her.

wrap see rap

wrapped see rapt

wreak see reek

wreck see reck

wrest see rest

wretch see retch

wright see right

wring see ring

write see right

wrote see rote

wrung see rung

wry see rye

Y

Y's see wise

yew see ewe

you see ewe

your see ewer

you're see ewer

Note: For an additional list of homophones less frequently used, see Part III, pp. 63–69.

Part II

A DICTIONARY OF HOMOGRAPHS

(Pairs of words that have the same spellings but with
different pronunciations and different meanings)

aged¹ (rhymes with raged; one-syllable word) past tense of **age**, grow old:— How Grandfather has aged in the past six months!

aged² (rhymes with cage hid; accent on the first syllable) very old:—That aged woman recently celebrated her ninetieth birthday.

arch¹ (rhymes with bark) a prefix meaning chief as in **archangel**.

arch² (rhymes with march) 1. a bow:— The rainbow is in the form of an arch. 2. a curved portal:—The Arc de Triumph is an arch.

ate¹ (rhymes with late) past tense of **eat**:—We ate eight cookies.

Ate² (rhymes with Katie) Greek goddess of punishment.

August¹ (rhymes with dog must; accent on the first syllable) the eighth month of the year:—We usually vacation in August and go to the beach.

august² (rhymes with sawdust; accent on the second syllable) majestic:— The Pope's august presence graced the ceremony.

bases¹ (rhymes with cases) plural of **base**, a foundation or a position in the game of baseball:—The fielder caught the flyball and put out two men on bases.

bases² (rhymes with Macy's) plural of **basis**, a foundation:—Those new houses rest securely on their bases.

bass¹ (rhymes with face) 1. the lower-pitched part of vocal or instrumental music, also a male singer with a very low voice:—The bass singers in Russian choirs are famous.

bass² (rhymes with mass) 1. an edible fish:—We caught a striped bass near a waterfall. 2. a kind of hardwood tree:—That chair is made of bass wood.

blessed¹ (rhymes with rest; a one-syllable word) past tense of **bless**, commend another person to God:— During the mass the priest blessed the congregation.

blessed² (rhymes with dress hid: accent on the first syllable) holy:—The Blessed Mary is revered by all Catholics.

bow¹ (rhymes with go) 1. a knot in a string, rope, or ribbon with two loops:—I like bow ties on men. 2. a curved stick used in archery:—Little George plays Indian with his bow and arrow. Compare **beau**.

bow² (rhymes with now) 1. incline the head as a mark of respect:—In church during prayers the worshippers bow their heads. 2. the front end of a boat or ship:—George Washington is pictured as standing in the bow of a ship while crossing the Delaware River.

bower¹ (rhymes with goer) a musician that uses a bow in order to play a stringed instrument:—That violinist is a good bower.

bower² (rhymes with power) an outdoor shady, leafy place, an arbor or shelter:—The lovers were screened from observation by a bower.

buffet¹ (rhymes with stuff it, accent on the first syllable) hit, strike, knock: —You should have seen the stormy waves buffet our ship.

buffet² (rhymes with rough day, accent on the second syllable) 1. a sideboard in a dining-room:—We keep our large silver set on the buffet. 2. said of meals not served at tables but eaten with the plate in one's lap:—Our church served a buffet supper.

cater¹ (rhymes with later) 1. attend to, serve:—Ellen's mother will always cater to her daughter's every whim. 2. serve meals at social functions:—Sherry's will cater at that wedding reception.

cater² (rhymes with batter) diagonal:—We live cater-cornered to our neighbors the Browns.

close¹ (rhymes with dose) 1. near:—The Whites live very close to us. 2. airless:—Open the window: it's too close in here.

close² (rhymes with goes) shut:—I was so sleepy I had to close my eyes.

collect¹ (rhymes with rollicked; accent on the first syllable) prayers repeated by the congregation as part of a church service:—After the hymn the dean read the collect.

collect² (rhymes with select; accent on the second syllable) 1. gather, assemble together:—After the show I went to the checkroom to collect my hat and coat. 2. obtain payment of a bill:—Since my debtor refused to pay what he owed me, I had to hire a lawyer to collect it.

colon¹ (rhymes with stolen) two dots (:) used in punctuation before a quotation, etc.:—Use a colon before a listing of various items.

Colon² (rhymes with Go, John: accent on the second syllable) eastern seaport of Panama:—The Panama Canal goes through Colon.

commune¹ (rhymes with psalm tune; accent on the first syllable) the smallest political division in Switzerland, France, or Italy:—That political leader came from an obscure commune.

commune² (rhymes with a tune; accent on the second syllable) converse with:—In church we commune with God.

compact¹ (rhymes with bomb cracked; accent on the first syllable) 1. a formal agreement:—The passengers on the Mayflower made a solemn compact. 2. a lady's powder box or tin:—Mary carries a gold-plated compact in her purse.

compact² (rhymes with come stacked; accent on the second syllable) well arranged as to efficient use of space, close fitting:—Our compact bed folds up and may be stored in our car.

conduct¹ (rhymes with Don ducked; accent on the first syllable) behavior, actions:—I was surprised at his unusual conduct in coming to the office unshaven.

conduct² (rhymes with unshucked; accent on the second syllable) 1. lead an orchestra, guide a group, etc.:—The teachers often conduct their pupils through the museum. 2. act as a passage for:—Wires conduct electricity into our house.

conjure¹ (rhymes with manure; accent on the first syllable) beg or implore one to do something:—I conjure you to keep your promise to support your widowed mother.

conjure² (rhymes with ensure: accent on the second syllable) do a trick, work magic:—I saw that magician conjure a rabbit out of a hat.

conserve¹ (rhymes with Don serve; accent on the first syllable) a thick fruit jelly or jam:—We had conserves with our meat course.

conserve² (rhymes with unnerve; accent on the second syllable) save, store away for future use:—I went to bed early in order to conserve my strength for a hard day at the office.

console¹ (rhymes with Don stole; accent on the first syllable) keyboard, stops, etc. of a pipe organ:—The organist sits at the console and plays.

console² (rhymes with unroll; accent on the second syllable) make an unhappy person feel better, comfort, sympathize with:—A new puppy will console Carol for the loss of her old dog.

consort¹ (rhymes with Don's fort; accent on the first syllable) a queen's husband who is not a hereditary monarch:—Queen Victoria's husband was called the Prince Consort.

consort² (rhymes with a court; accent on the second syllable) associate with:—Mr. Baker objected to his son's tendency to consort with thieves.

content¹ (rhymes with convent; accent on the first syllable) whatever is inside a box, book, room, etc.:—The editorial content of that magazine is of wide interest.

content² (rhymes with invent; accent on the second syllable) happy, satisfied:—I am very content with my new job.

contract¹ (rhymes with Don lacked; accent on the first syllable) an agreement such as to buy and sell a certain article:—A has a contract with B to sell B his car.

contract² (rhymes with unpacked; accent on the second syllable) shrink, become smaller:—Metal contracts in the cold and expands in the heat.

desert¹ (rhymes with says Bert; accent on the first syllable) a hot, dry, treeless, sandy region:—The camel is called the ship of the desert.

desert² (rhymes with alert; accent on the second syllable) 1. abandon, leave, forsake:—She's afraid her husband will desert her for another woman. 2. that which should be justly given or received by a certain person:—Imprisonment was no more than that thief's just desert.

digest¹ (rhymes with buy best; accent on the first syllable) a condensed summary of a longer literary work:—"The Reader's Digest" is a collection of digests of longer articles in other magazines.

digest² (rhymes with molest; accent on

the second syllable) properly assimilate one's food after eating:—Father cannot digest pork.

do¹ (rhymes with shoe) act, perform, accomplish:—I'm going to do my homework.

do² (rhymes with go) the first tone of the musical solfege scale:—Re, mi, fa, and sol come after do in the ascending scale.

does¹ (rhymes with buzz) third person singular of do, perform:—That carpenter does his work well.

does² (rhymes with goes) two or more female deer:—In the woods I saw a buck and three does.

dove¹ (rhymes with love, glove) a small bird, a pigeon:—The dove is a symbol of peace.

dove² (rhymes with stove) past tense of dive, plunge:—Jack dove off the high springboard into the water.

entrance¹ (accent on the first syllable) a door, gate, or other opening to a building, room, park, etc., opposite of exit:—There is a revolving door at the entrance to that restaurant.

entrance² (rhymes with a dance, accent on the second syllable) hold spellbound, greatly interest or appeal to:—That ballerina can always entrance her audience.

excuse¹ (rhymes with thick juice, accent on the second syllable) a reason given for doing something objectionable or for failing to do something usually expected:—Charles's excuse for being late was that the bus had broken down.

excuse² (rhymes with fix fuse) 1. let someone off a task or duty:—Because of her illness the teacher will excuse Alice from class early. 2. pardon:—Please excuse my clumsiness in stepping on your foot.

forte¹ (rhymes with sort) what one can do well:—Good cooking is that woman's forte.

forte² (rhymes with forty) played very loud, said of music:—The horns played that passage forte.

gallant¹ (rhymes with talent; accent on the first syllable) brave, chivalrous: —That gallant fireman led three trapped householders out of the flaming building.

gallant² (rhymes with the plant, accent on the second syllable) 1. a man especially attentive to women, a flatterer:—See that beauty and her gallants. 2. (adj.) chivalrous to women: —Sam is very gallant and pays those attentions to women which most men skip.

gill¹ (rhymes with mill; G as in George) a liquid measure:—Four gills equal one pint.

gill² (rhymes with mill; G as in guess) the breathing apparatus of a fish:— The fisherman hooked a fish under its gills.

he'll¹ (rhymes with meal) contraction of he will:—When John promises to do something, he'll perform it.

hell² (rhymes with bell) the place below the earth for punishing lost souls:— Christians believe a man's soul goes either to heaven or to hell.

herb¹ (rhymes with curb; the H is silent) a type of green plant used for flavoring foods or for medicinal purposes:—Mint is an herb used in drinks or with meat.

Herb² (rhymes with curb; the H is pronounced) short for **Herbert**, a boy's name.

hinder¹ (rhymes with tinder) prevent temporarily or permanently, place obstacles in one's path:—The fact that I have only 25 cents will hinder me from buying a watch.

hinder² (rhymes with binder) pertaining to the rear part, especially of an animal, opposite of **fore:**—That horse has a bad bruise in his hinder parts.

incense¹ (rhymes with win hens); accent on the first syllable) perfume burned in a dish or pot:—Incense was burned before the holy altar.

incense² (rhymes with intense; accent on the second syllable) make angry: —The passengers were incensed by the rudeness of the bus-driver.

intern¹ (rhymes with shin burn; accent on the first syllable) a recent graduate in medicine serving as an assistant doctor in a hospital:—The patient's regular doctor left instructions with the staff intern.

intern² (rhymes with in turn; accent on the second syllable) hold, keep, or segregate citizens or property belonging to another nation during wartime, etc.:—During World War II Germans' property within the United States was interned.

intimate¹ (rhymes with begin to date) hint, tell indirectly:—I heard John intimate that his chief is being appointed to a high position by the President.

intimate² (rhymes with hint a bit) closely bound together, in a close relationship:—Yes, those two women are very intimate.

invalid¹ (rhymes with win the bid; accent on the first syllable) an ill and often disabled person:—After she became eighty, grandmother became an invalid for the rest of her life.

invalid² (rhymes with in salad; accent on the second syllable) worthless, useless:—The deceased's will was invalid because it had not been signed or witnessed.

Job¹ (rhymes with robe) a character in the Old Testament who had many misfortunes:—The Book of Job is in the Bible.

job² (rhymes with rob) 1. a position, work, or employment:—Tom has a job in the postoffice. 2. a particular piece of work:—The mechanic did a swell job on my car.

lead¹ (rhymes with speed) conduct:— Mr. Morton, our choirmaster, leads the choir. I have to lead my dog on a leash.

lead² (rhymes with bed) the common heavy soft metal, also the graphite in a pencil with which one writes: —Lead is used by plumbers in the form of lead pipe. Cf. **led.**

Levy¹ a surname (rhymes with Stevie).

levy² (rhymes with heavy) tax, charge:—The Government will levy on all imports of a certain kind.

live¹ (rhymes with give) inhabit, reside, be alive:—I live in Boston. Washington happened to live in the eighteenth century.

live² (rhymes with drive) not dead, alive:—The hunters caught a live lion for the zoo. When electricity flows through a wire, that wire is a live wire.

minute¹ (rhymes with pin it; accent on the first syllable) a period of sixty seconds, or a very short time in general:—One minute from now the President will speak on television.

minute² (rhymes with thin boot; accent on the second syllable) very small:—There were minute amounts of impurities in that drinking water.

mow¹ (rhymes with go) cut grass:—I must mow my lawn; the grass is getting too tall.

mow² (rhymes with how) a place in a barn for storing hay, a haymow:—On a summer afternoon it's hot in the mow.

Nice¹ (rhymes with peace) a city in Southern France:—We sunned ourselves on the beach at Nice.

nice² (rhymes with ice) 1. a vague word expressing approval:—We had a nice time at the seashore last summer. 2. discriminative:—The professor made a nice distinction between the words "happy" and "fortunate."

object¹ (rhymes with Rob licked; accent on the first syllable) 1. something with three dimensions:—A potato is a familiar-looking object in the kitchen. 2. receiver:—Mary was the object of Henry's attention.

object² (rhymes with affect; accent on the second syllable) express dislike or opposition to:—Some husbands object to their wives' extravagance.

pate¹ (rhymes with late) the head:—That old man's pate is as white as snow.

pâté² (rhymes with that day; accent on the second syllable) a paste made of finely ground meat:—Pâté de foie gras is a great delicacy.

patent¹ (rhymes with latent) obvious, clear:—It was patent that the President didn't want to run for a second term although he had made no direct statement to that effect.

patent² (rhymes with cat hunt) a document from the federal government giving the inventor exclusive rights to manufacture and market his invention:—Edison obtained many patents in his lifetime.

permit¹ (rhymes with hermit, accent on the first syllable) an official paper or document giving the holder permission to build a house, drive a car, etc.:—Before you learn to drive a car you must get a learner's permit.

permit² (rhymes with her fit; accent on the second syllable) allow, give permission:—I won't permit my young son to watch television all day.

Polish¹ (rhymes with stole dish; accent on the first syllable) pertaining to the country of Poland:—Chopin was Polish.

polish² (rhymes with abolish) 1. shine or brighten up metal or leather:—I just had my muddy shoes polished. 2. social grace:—That young man has lots of polish.

poll¹ (rhymes with hole) secure votes on a measure or project:—That soap company will poll many housewives on their preferences for soap.

Poll² (rhymes with doll) short for a girl's name **Polly**, a name often given to a parrot:—Poor Poll, our parrot, can only speak a few choice swear words.

present¹ (rhymes with pleasant; accent on the first syllable) 1. a gift:—I gave Mother a present for her birthday. 2. not absent:—Joan was present in class today. 3. now, the current time:—We all live in the present.

present² (rhymes with a tent; accent on the second syllable) 1. give:—They will present the retiring employee with a gold watch. 2. introduce:—May I present my wife?

primer¹ (rhymes with simmer) a school textbook for a very young child or other beginner:—"The New England Primer" is a famous early American printed book.

primer² (rhymes with climber) 1. a substance such as gasoline used to start a cold engine:—I must use a primer if I am going to get my car started. 2. an undercoat of paint applied before the second coat.

project¹ (rhymes with Dodge wrecked; accent on the first syllable) a plan or proposal:—What do you think of the project to harness the ocean tides in order to produce electric power?

project² (accent on the second syllable) 1. throw or hurl:—That cannon can project a missile thirty miles. 2. stretch out beyond:—That overhanging roof projects out over the attic windows.

read¹ (rhymes with need) 1. peruse a book, magazine, or newspaper silently:—I can read French easily. 2. speak aloud the words of a book or other printed or handwritten matter:—Our teacher often reads literary passages to us.

read² (rhymes with bed) past tense of read¹, peruse written or printed matter:—When we were small children, Mother often read to us.

record¹ (rhymes with checkered; accent on the first syllable) 1. a writing down, a note made:—We have a record of our last year's expenses. 2. a phonograph disc:—Our machine plays two sizes of records. 3. the highest mark or achievement:—Last year a record was reached in outdoor movie attendance.

record² (rhymes with reward; accent on the second syllable) make note of, write down, make an oral recording:—Columbia Records will record her voice.

refuse¹ (rhymes with deaf goose; accent on the first syllable) trash, garbage, or other waste material:—We have an incinerator in which we burn all our refuse.

refuse² (rhymes with bemuse; accent on the second syllable) decline to do or to accept; say no:—John's parents refuse to buy their son a motorcycle.

retail¹ (rhymes with tea sale; accent on the first syllable) 1. sell a product directly to the public or consumer:—That store retails shoes. 2. Also as adjective:—That store is a retail outlet. That is a retail store.

retail² (rhymes with regale; accent on the second syllable) retell or pass on news about an incident, repeat scandal:—Old Mrs. Jones is likely to retail all the local gossip to anyone who will listen.

row¹ (rhymes with go) 1. line of chairs, etc.:—In our class I sit in the second row. 2. propel a boat by oars:—When we were small children, we learned to row a small boat.

row² (rhymes with now) a fuss, fight or quarrel:—When Mr. Smith came home drunk, he had a terrible row with his wife.

seer¹ (rhymes with beer) a prophet, one who foresees events:—A seer warned the Trojans not to receive the wooden horse.

seer² (rhymes with freer, comparative of free) one who sees:—A sight-seer is a tourist who wants to see the sights. Broadway is thronged with sight-seers.

sewer¹ (rhymes with brewer, doer) an underground passage used to carry off waste:—Our drain-pipes empty into the sewer under the street.

sewer² (rhymes with goer, mower) one who sews with needle and thread:—Mother is a very neat sewer. See sewer³—sower

she'd¹ (rhymes with need) contraction of she would or she had (better):—Afternoons she'd often stop at the drug-store for a sundae. She'd better study harder if she expects to pass her geometry.

shed² (rhymes with bed) a building behind the main house and used for storage, often open in front:—We keep our garden tools in the toolshed.

shower¹ (rhymes with blower) one who shows or demonstrates:—That shower of rugs is an Armenian.

shower² (rhymes with power) 1. a spray of falling water:—Our bathroom has a tub and a fixture for a shower. 2. a party in honor of an engaged girl:—Martha received many useful presents for her future home during a shower given her by her best friend.

singer¹ (rhymes with ringer; ng as in bring) one who sings:—There are twelve singers in that church choir.

singer² (rhymes with ginger) one who singes, scorches, or burns slightly:—A barber is often a singer of his customer's hair which he singes in order to promote its growth.

slaver¹ (rhymes with favor) one who enslaves and sells human beings, also the ship on which such unfortunates were transported:—At the end of the Civil War most American slavers were put out of business.

slaver² (rhymes with have her) drip saliva from the mouth:—A dog will often slaver at the expectation of food.

sow¹ (rhymes with go) plant or scatter seed in the ground:—We farmers sow our wheat in the fall.

sow² (rhymes with now) a mature female pig:—Our old sow has just given birth to 16 piglets.

stingy¹ (rhymes with stringy; ng as in bring) said of a prickling or stinging sensation:—Ginger ale or other carbonated drinks offer the drinker a stingy taste.

stingy² (rhymes with dingy, G as in George) ungenerous, miserly:—Martha's escort was too stingy to take her to the movies.

subject¹ (rhymes with cub kicked; accent on the first syllable) 1. what one is discussing, the theme:—The subject of the lecture was freedom of speech. 2. under the power, control, or influence of:—That great king was kind to his subjects. That agreement is subject to review by the Board.

subject² (rhymes with correct; accent on the second syllable) cause one to undergo a hardship or difficulty:—How can Tom subject himself to his employer's insults?

tarry¹ (rhymes with carry) wait, stay, remain behind:—Sorry I can't tarry any longer. I must leave because I have a dental appointment in fifteen minutes.

tarry² (rhymes with sorry, starry) sticky, covered with black tar:—Drive slowly on this tarry road. The surface hasn't dried yet.

tear¹ (rhymes with fear) a natural drop of water from the eye-ducts:—A tear rolled down Mary's cheek after she tore her dress on a nail.

tear² (rhymes with care) rip apart:—I must tear out that recipe from the woman's page.

tier¹ (rhymes with fear) one of several levels or layers:—That cake has three tiers. Our seats were in the third tier at the opera. See **tear¹**

tier² (rhymes with buyer) one who ties or fastens:—That boy scout won a medal as a tier of knots. See **tire**

transfer¹ (rhymes with fans her; accent on the first syllable) a paper slip given by a bus driver to a passenger who wishes to take a connecting bus without paying an additional fare:—When I paid my fare, I asked the driver for a transfer to the crosstown bus.

transfer² (rhymes with and her; accent on the second syllable) change from one place to another:—My husband's firm will transfer him from Chicago to New York.

use¹ (rhymes with goose) the disposition, employment, or service of:—To what use do you put old newspapers and rags? Do you have any use for stale bread?

use² (rhymes with news) employ, adopt:—Do you use an electric razor or an old-fashioned one?

vice¹ (rhymes with twice) 1. a bad habit or moral sin:—Smoking is a minor vice, but adultery is a major one. 2. second in command or acting in place of the officer named:—Jack is a vice-president of his father's company.

vice² (rhymes with icy) in place of:—Smith now heads the State Department vice Brown, who just retired.

we'd¹ (rhymes with need) contraction of we had or we would:—If we'd studied harder, we'd have won the prizes.

wed² (rhymes with bed) marry:—When did George wed Mary?

we'll¹ (rhymes with feel) contraction of we will:—We'll help you pack.

well² (rhymes with sell) 1. a deep hole dug in the ground to collect water and from which water is obtained:—They pump their water from a well. 2. not sick or ill, in good health:—I feel well. 3. an exclamation or surprise, etc.:—Well! Ken is certainly getting fat. 4. excellently, satisfactorily:—Charles did well in his exam.

wind¹ (rhymes with pinned) 1. a current of air:—A cold wind made a very chilly Easter Day. 2. exhaust, leave breathless:—A quick run usually winds me.

wind² (rhymes with kind) twist or turn:—His wife is so dominant that she can wind him around her little finger. Every morning I wind the clock (tighten the mainspring by turning).

won't¹ (rhymes with don't) contraction of will not:—She won't pass her exam because she won't study for it.

wont² (rhymes with hunt) 1. habit or custom:—Yesterday Jim read the newspaper on the train as was his wont. 2. used to, accustomed to:—Martha was wont to sleep late on Sunday mornings.

wound¹ (rhymes with tuned) 1. inflict a cut, puncture, or gash in a person's body, also the injury itself:—In the scuffle the policeman managed to wound the attacking thief. 2. hurt one's feelings:—His harsh words about her ugliness wound her.

wound² (rhyme with found) past tense of **wind**, twist or turn:—Mary wound the silk kerchief around her head.

Note: A list of 60 less frequently used homographs is given on p. 69.

Part III

A LIST OF
800 ADDITIONAL HOMOPHONES LESS FREQUENTLY USED

(Note: Terms marked with an asterisk (*) or a superior number give equivalent pronunciations and are to be found in Parts I and II)

A

Acadian—Akkadian
accede—exceed
access—excess
accessary—accessory
accessory, see accessary
accidence—accidents
accidents, see accidence
acclamation—acclimation
acclimation, see acclamation
accord—a cord
a cord, see accord
a curd—occurred
a dew, see *adieu—ado
adherence—adherents
adherents, see adherence
adolescence—adolescents
adolescents, see adolescence
aerial—Ariel
aerie—aery—airy
aery, see aerie
aims—Ames
airy, see aerie
Akkadian, see Acadian
albumen—albumin
albumin, see albumen
align—a line
a line, see align
amerce—immerse
Ames, see aims
ana—Anna
analyst—annalist
Anna, see ana
annalist, see analyst
annunciate—enunciate
antecedence—antecedents
antecedents, see antecedence
apprize—a prize
a prize, see apprize
a rain—arraign
Ariel, see aerial
arraign, see a rain
arrant—errant

Asch—ash
ash, see Asch
Ate[2]—eighty
Auer, see *hour—our
aureole—oriole
auricle—oracle
ay, see *a—eh
Ayr, see *air—ere—heir

B

B's—bees
Baal, see *bail—bale
Bach—bock—Bok
bait—bate
baize—bays—beys
balled, see *bald—bawled
bank—banque
banque, see bank
barber—Barbour
Barbour, see barber
baring—bearing—Bering
bark—barque
Barney—barny
barny, see Barney
barque, see bark
Barre—Barrie—Barry,
   see *berry—bury
Barrie, see Barre
Barry, see Barre
bat—batt
bate, see bait
baton—batten
batt, see bat
batten, see baton
Bauer, see *bower[2]
bay—bey
bays, see baize
bead—Bede
bearing, see baring
beaut—Butte
Bede, see bead
bees, see B's
beetle—betel
Bering, see baring

Bernie—byrnie
betel, see beetle
bey, see bay
beys, see baize
bird—Byrd
Bloch, see *bloc—block
Blount—blunt
blunt, see Blount
Bo, see *beau—bow[1]
bock, see Bach
Boer—Bohr—boor,
   see *boar—bore
bogey—bogy
bogy, see bogey
Bohr, see Boer
boil—Boyle
Bok, see Bach
boles—bolls—Bowles—bowls
bolled, see *bold—bowled
bolls, see boles
boon—Boone
Boone, see boon
boor, see Boer
boro, see *borough—burro
boroughs—burros—
   Burroughs—burrows
bower,[2] see Bauer
bowlder, see *bolder—
   boulder
Bowles, see boles
bowls, see boles
Boyle, see boil
brae—bray
braes, see *braise—brays—
   braze
brag—Bragg
Bragg, see brag
bray, see brae
breast—Brest
Brest, see breast
briar—brier
brier, see briar
brighten—Brighton
Brighton, see brighten

63

Britain—Briton
Briton, see Britain
broom—Broome
Broome, see broom
brut, see *bruit—brute
bunion—Bunyan
Bunyan, see bunion
Burghley—Burleigh—Burley—burly
Burleigh, see Burghley
Burley, see Burghley
burly, see Burghley
burros, see boroughs
Burroughs, see boroughs
burrows, see boroughs
Busch—bush
bush, see Busch
Butte, see beaut
buyer—byre
Byrd, see bird
byre, see buyer
byrnie, see Bernie

C

Caesar—seize her
Cain's—canes—Keynes
Caius—keys
calix—calyx
calk—caulk
call—caul
callous—callus
callus, see callous
calm it—comet
calyx, see calix
camel—Campbell
Campbell, see camel
canes, see Cain's
canine—K 9
cantaloupe—can't elope
can't elope, see cantaloupe
canter—cantor
cantor, see canter
car—Carr—Kerr
Carey—carry—Cary
caries—carries
Carlisle—Carlyle
Carlyle, see Carlisle
carol—carrel
Carr, see car
carrel, see carol
carries, see caries
carry, see Carey
Cary, see Carey
caudal—caudle
caudle, see caudal
caul, see call
caulk, see calk
Cecil—sessile
ceil—seal—seel
center—sent her
cere, see *sear—seer—sere
chain—Cheyne
Chan's, see *chance—chants
chapel—Chappell
Chappell, see chapel
chard—charred
charred, see chard
check off—Chekov
Chekov, see check off
cheque, see *check—Czech
Cheyne, see chain
choir, in choir—enquire—inquire
Chrysler—Kreisler
chyl—Kyle
Ciceley—Sisley
Cid—Sid—Syd
cinque—sink
cist—cyst
claimant—clamant
clamant, see claimant
Claude—clawed
Claus, see *clause—claws
clawed, see Claude
clay—Klee
Cleaves—Cleves
Cleves, see Cleaves
clew—clue
click—clique
climber—Clymer
clique, see click
clue, see clew
Clymer, see climber
Coad—code
coalman—Colman
coaming—combing
coarser—courser
coat—cote
Cobh—cove
cocks—Cox
coddling—codling
code, see Coad
codling, see coddling
coign—coin—quoin
coin, see coign
cola—kola
Collier—Collyer
Collyer, see Collier
Colman, see coalman
color—culler
combing, see coaming
comet, see calm it
complacence—complaisance
complaisance, see complacence
con—Kahn—Khan
conch—conk
confidante—confident
confident, see confidante
conk, see conch
consonance—consonants
consonants, see consonance
continence—continents
continents, see continence
Cooley, see *coolie—coolly
Cooper—Cowper
copy—kopje
correspondence—correspondents
correspondents, see correspondence
corse, see *coarse—course
cote, see coat
councillor—counsellor
counsellor, see councillor
courser, see coarser
cove, see Cobh
Cowes—cows
Cowper, see Cooper
cows, see Cowes
Cox, see cocks
crab—Crabbe
Crabbe, see crab
craft—kraft
creases, in creases—increases
cress—Kress
Cretan—cretin
cretin, see Cretan
crewel—cruel
cruel, see crewel
cruse, see *crews—cruise
culler, see color
curd, a curd—occurred
Cy—psi—sigh
cygnet—signet
cypress—Cyprus
Cyprus, see cypress
cyst, see cist

D

D—dee
daemon—demon
daily—Daly
Daly, see daily
Dane—deign
Day—dey
dean—dene
dee, see D
deign, see Dane

demean—demesne
demesne, see demean
demon, see daemon
dene, see dean
descendant—descendent
descendent, see descendant
dew, a dew, see*adieu—ado
Dewey—dewy
dews—dues
dewy, see Dewey
dey, see day
di, see *die—dye
diarist—direst
Dick's—Dix
dine—dyne
dire—dyer
direst, see diarist
disc—disk
discreet—discrete
discrete, see discreet
disk, see disc
Dix, see Dick's
Donne, see *done—dun
dost—dust
double you—w
Doug—dug
drachm—dram
draft—draught
dram, see drachm
draught, see draft
drei—dry
dries—drys
droop—drupe
drupe, see droop
dry, see drei
drys, see dries
dues, see dews
dug, see Doug
dust, see dost
dyer, see dire
dyne, see dine

E

earn—Ern
eaten—Eaton—Eton
Eaton, see eaten
eel—'e'll
e'er, see *air—ere—heir
eerie—Erie
eighty, see Ate²
elicit—illicit
ell—L
e'll, see eel
Elsie—l.c.
em—M
enclose—inclose
endorse—indorse

enquire, see choir, in choir
enunciate, see annunciate
Erie, see eerie
Ern, see earn
errant, see arrant
eruption—irruption
Eton, see eaten
exceed, see accede
excess, see access

F

faerie, see *fairy—ferry
fail—faille
faille, see fail
faker—fakir
fakir, see faker
faro—Faroe—Pharoah
Faroe, see faro
faucet—Fawcett
Fawcett, see fáucet
fay—fey
fays, see *faze—phase
feed—fee'd
fee'd, see feed
felloe—fellow
fellow, see felloe
feud—few'd
few'd, see feud
fey, see fay
fife—Phyfe
firs—furse
Fischer, see *fisher—fissure
fizz—phiz
flag—Flagg
Flagg, see flag
flecks—flex
flex, see flecks
Flo, see *floe—flow
formally—formerly
formerly, see formally
fouler—fowler
fowler, see fouler
Fries, see *frees—freeze—
   frieze
fro—frow
frow, see fro
furnace—Furnas—Furness
Furnas, see furnace
Furness, see furnace
furse, see firs

G

Gael—Gail—gale
gage—gauge
Gail, see Gael
gale, see Gael
gall—Gaul

gallop—Gallup—galop
Gallup, see gallop
galop, see gallop
gang—gangue
gangue, see gang
gaol—jail
gauge, see gage
Gaul, see gall
genes—Gene's—jeans—Jean's
gent—Ghent
Gert—girt
gest—jest
Ghent, see gent
gilder—guilder
girt, see Gert
glair—glare
glare, see glair
glows—gloze
gloze, see glows
gnash—Nash
gnat—Nat
gneiss, see *nice²
gnome—Nome
gnu, see *knew—new
goo—gout¹
gout,¹ see goo
gram—gramme
gramme, see gram
grater—greater
gray—grey
greater, see grater
greaves—grieves
grewsome—gruesome
grey, see gray
grieves, see greaves
griffin—griffon
griffon, see griffin
groat—Grote
grocer—grosser
grosgrain—grow grain
grosser, see grocer
Grote, see groat
grow grain, see grosgrain
gruesome, see grewsome
guilder, see gilder
gyve—jive

H

Hague—Haig
Haig, see Hague
Handel—handle
handle, see Handel
hands—Hans
Hans, see hands
harts—Hartz—hearts
Harty—hearty
Hartz, see harts

haws—hawse
hawse, see haws
hearts, see harts
hearty, see Harty
heaum—holm—home
height—hight
her suit—hirsute
Herr, see *hair—hare
Hertz—hurts
hews—Hughes—Hugh's
hight, see height
hirsute, see her suit
hissed—hist
hist, see hissed
ho—hoe
hoe, see ho
hold—holed
holed, see hold
holey, see *holy—wholly
holm, see heaum
Holmes—homes
home, see heaum
homes, see Holmes
Hughes, see hews
Hugh's, see hews
Hurd, see *heard—herd
hurts, see Hertz
Hyman—hymen
hymen, see Hyman

I

I deal—ideal
ideal, see I deal
illicit, see elicit
immanent—imminent
immerse, see ammerce
imminent, see immanent
in choir, see choir, in choir
incidence—incidents
incidents, see incidence
incite—in sight
inclose, see enclose
in creases—increases
increases, see creases,
  in creases
indorse, see endorse
inquire, see choir, in choir
in sight, see incite
inure—in your
in your, see inure
IOU—I owe you
I owe you, see IOU
irruption, see eruption

J

jail, see gaol
jeans, see genes

Jean's, see genes
jest, see gest
jive, see gyve
John—Jon
Johnson—Jonson
Jon, see John
Jonson, see Johnson
Juvenal—juvenile
juvenile, see Juvenal

K

K—Kay
K 9, see canine
Kahn, see con
Kaiser—Keyser
Kane, see *Cain—cane
Kant, see *cant—can't
Kay, see K
Kean—keen—Keene
keel—Kiel
keen, see Kean
Keene, see Kean
kein—kine
Kerr, see car
Kew, see *cue—queue
Keynes, see Cain's
keys, see Caius
Keyser, see Kaiser
Khan, see con
kid—Kidd—Kyd
Kidd, see kid
Kiel, see keel
kine, see kein
Klee, see clay
Knapp—nap
kneel—Neale—Neil
knicker—nicker
knit—nit
knob—nob
knobby—nobby
knocks—Knox—nox
Knolls—Knowles
Knowles, see Knolls
Knox, see knocks
kola, see cola
kopje, see copy
kraft, see craft
Kreisler, see Chrysler
Kress, see cress
Kyd, see kid
Kyle, see chyl

L

L, see ell
lac—lack
laches—latches
lack, see lac

lacker—lacquer
lacquer, see lacker
lacs, see *lacks—lax
lam—lamb
lama—llama
lamb, see lam
lap—Lapp
Lapp, see lap
latches, see laches
Latin—latten
latten, see Latin
laud—lawed
Laurie—lorry
lawed, see laud
l.c., see Elsie
leads¹—Leeds
leas—Lee's—lees
Lear—leer
leave—lieve
Leeds, see leads¹
leer, see Lear
lees, see leas
Lee's, see leas
Leif, see *leaf—lief
Leigh, see *lea—lee
leman—lemon
lemon, see leman
let—Lett
Lett, see let
Lettice—lettuce
lettuce, see Lettice
Lew—lieu—loo—Lou
lichen—liken
lieu, see Lew
lieve, see leave
liken, see lichen
lily—Lyly
limb—limn
lime—Lyme
limn, see limb
line, a line, see align
links—lynx
list—Liszt
Liszt, see list
literal—littoral
littoral, see literal
llama, see lama
loo, see Lew
loon—lune
loose—Luce
lorry, see Laurie
Lou, see Lew
Luce, see loose
lune, see loon
Lyly, see lily
Lyme, see lime
lynx, see links

M

M, see em
Mack's—Max
Mae—may
Magdalen—maudlin
manual—Manuel
Manuel, see manual
mar—Meagher
mark—marque
marque, see mark
marquee—marquis
marquis, see marquee
marten—Martin
Martin, see marten
mat—Matt—matte
Matt, see mat
matte, see mat
maudlin, see Magdalen
Max, see Mack's
may, see Mae
Meade, see *mead—meed
Meagher, see mar
Mede, see Meade
meet her, see *meeter—
    meter
Merck—murk
mesne, see *mean—mien
Meyer—mire—Myer
mica—Micah
Micah, see mica
micks—mix
Migne, see *mean—mien
mill—Milne
millenary—millinery
millinery, see millenary
Milne, see mill
mire, see Meyer
mix, see micks
Moe—*mow¹—mot
Moore, see *moor—more
mordant—mordent
mordent, see mordant
More, see *moor—more
mot, see Moe
murk, see Merck
Myer, see Meyer

N

nap, see Knapp
Nash, see gnash
Nat, see gnat
naught—nought
Neale, see kneel
Neil, see kneel
Ney, see *nay—née—neigh
Nichols—nickels

nickels, see Nichols
nicker, see knicker
nicks—nix
nigh—Nye
nit, see knit
nix, see nicks
nob, see knob
nobby, see knobby
noise—Noyes
Nome, see gnome
nought, see naught
nox, see knocks
Noyes, see noise
Nye, see nigh

O

occurred, see a curd
once—wants
oppose—a pose
oppress—a press
oracle, see auricle
ordinance—ordnance
ordnance, see ordinance
Origen—origin
origin, see Origen
oriole, see aureole
ouse—use

P

packs—pax
Paine, see *pain—pane
palace—Pallas
Pallas, see palace
pan—panne
panne, see pan
parol—parole
parole, see parol
passed her—pastor
pastor, see passed her
patten—Patton
Patton, see patten
pax, see packs
Payne, see *pain-pane
peeps—Pepys
pekoe—picot
pelisse—police
pen—Penn
pencil—pensile
Penn, see pen
pensile, see pencil
Pepys, see peeps
père, see *pair—pare—pear
Pharaoh, see faro
phare, see *fair—fare
phiz, see fizz
Phyfe, see fife

pick it—picket—Pickett
picked—Pict
picket, see pick it
Pickett, see pick it
picks—pix—pyx
picot, see pekoe
Pict, see picked
pious—Pius
pistil—pistol
pistol, see pistil
pit—Pitt
Pitt, see pit
Pius, see pious
pix, see picks
place—plaice
place her—placer¹
placer¹, see place her
plaice, see place
plough—plow
plow, see plough
Po—Poe
pocks—pox
Poe, see Po
poke—Polk
police, see pelisse
Polk, see poke
pomace—pumice
pommel—pummel
populace—populous
populous, see populace
port—Porte
Porte, see port
pose, a pose, see oppose
pox, see pocks
precisian—precision
precision, see precisian
press, a press, see oppress
prier—prior—pryer—Pryor
primmer—*primer¹
prior, see prier
prise, see *pries—prize
prize, a prize, see apprize
Procter—proctor
proctor, see Procter
pryer, see prier
Pryor, see prier
psi, see *Cy—sigh
pumice, see pomace
pummel, see pommel
pyx, see picks

Q

quean—queen
queen, see quean
quoin, see coin

R

rabbet—rabbit
rabbit, see rabbet
rack—wrack
rack it—racket—racquet
racket, see rack it
racquet, see rack it
rain, a rain, see arraign
Reade, see *read[1]—reed
recede—re-seed
receipt—re-seat
Reece—Reese—Riis
Reese, see Reece
Reid, see *read[1]—reed
re-seat, see receipt
re-seed, see recede
Rex—wrecks
rheum—room
Rhodes—roads
Rhone—roan
rhumb—rum
rider—Ryder
Riis, see Reece
ritz—writs
roads, see Rhodes
roan, see Rhone
roc—rock
rock, see roc
roes, see *rose—rows[1]
Rolle, see *role—roll
room, see rheum
rum, see rhumb
Ryder, see rider
rye, see *a rye—awry

S

sacs—Sachs—sacks—Saks—
  sax
Sachs, see sacs
sacks, see sacs
saith—Seth
sake[2]—Saki
Saki, see sake[2]
Saks, see sacs
sands—sans
sane—Seine
sans, see sands
sax, see sacs
scald—skald
Schley—sly
scion—Sion
seal, see ceil
sects—sex
seel, see ceil
Seine, see sane
seize her, see Caesar

Senate—sennet—sennit
sennet, see Senate
sennit, see Senate
sent her, see center
seraph—serif
serif, see seraph
sessile, see Cecil
Seth, see saith
*sewer[1]—suer
sex, see sects
she'll—Shiel
Shelley—shelly
shelly, see Shelley
Shepard—Shepherd
Shepherd, see Shepard
shew—show
Shiel, see she'll
shire—shyer
show, see shew
shyer, see shire
sics—sicks—six
sicks, see sics
Sid, see Cid
sigh, see Cy
sight, in sight, see incite
signet, see cygnet
Simeon—simian
simian, see Simeon
sing—Synge
sink, see cinque
Sion, see scion
Sioux—sue—Sue
Sisley, see Ciceley
sits—sitz
sitz, see sits
six, see sics
skald, see scald
slew—slue
sloe—slow
slow, see sloe
slue, see slew
sly, see Schley
Somers—summers
Somme, see *some—sum
sonny—sunny
spade—spayed
spayed, see spade
spin it—spinet
spinet, see spin it
spits—spitz
spitz, see spits
steely—stele
stele, see steely
Stephens—Stevens
Stevens, see Stephens
stew—Stu
sticks—Styx

stoop—stoupe
stoupe, see stoop
Stu, see stew
Styx, see sticks
subtler—sutler
sue, Sue, see Sioux
suer, see *sewer[1]
summers, see Somers
sunny, see sonny
surplice—surplus
surplus, see surplice
sutler, see subtler
Syd, see Cid—Sid
Syng, see sing

T

tael, see *tail—tale
Tamar—tamer
tamer, see Tamar
taper—tapir
tapir, see taper
taupe—tope
tern—turn
Thai—tie
the (str.)—thee
thee, see the
thru, see *threw—through
thyme—time
ti, see *T—tea
tie, see Thai
tiler—Tyler
timber—timbre
timbre, see timber
time, see thyme
tine—Tyne
tole—toll
toll, see tole
tope, see taupe
tor—tore
tore, see tor
tray—trey
trey, see tray
tricks—Trix
Trix, see tricks
trollop—Trollope
Trollope, see trollop
turn, see tern
Tyler, see tiler
Tyne, see tine
tyre, see *tier[2]—tire

U

use, see ouse

W

w, see double you
wail—wale
wails—Wales

waiver—waver
wale, see wail
Wales, see wails
wall—waul
wants, see once
war—wore
waul, see wall
waver, see waiver
weald—wield
wean—ween
weather—wether—whether
web—Webb

Webb, see web
ween, see wean
weir—we're
we're, see weir
wether, see weather
wheal—wheel
wheel, see wheal
whether, see weather
whew, see *hew—hue—
    Hugh
whirl—whorl
whorl, see whirl

wield, see weald
wolf—Wolfe—Woolf
Wolfe, see wolf
Woolf, see wolf
wore, see war
wrack, see rack
wrecks, see Rex
writs, see ritz

Y

your, in your, see inure

A List of 60 Additional Homographs

bowed[1]	leading[1]	Rachel[1]
bowed[2]	leading[2]	rachel[2]
converse[1]	lineage[1]	re[1]
converse[2]	lineage[2]	re[2]
convert[1]	lower[1]	ravel[1]
convert[2]	lower[2]	Ravel[2]
denier[1]	natal[1]	relay[1]
denier[2]	Natal[2]	relay[2]
Dives[1]	pasty[1]	said[1]
dives[2]	pasty[2]	Said[2]
frequent[1]	perfect[1]	shell[1]
frequent[2]	perfect[2]	she'll[2]
fries[1]	piano[1]	swinger[1]
Fries[2]	piano[2]	swinger[2]
gout[1]	placer[1]	Thais[1]
gout[2]	placer[2]	Thais[2]
ill[1]	putter[1]	ton[1]
I'll[2]	putter[2]	ton[2]
kinder[1]	prayer[1]	vale[1]
kinder[2]	prayer[2]	vale[2]

Part IV

EXERCISES

Note: Part IV is designed to test the student's knowledge and use of representative homophones and homographs, chiefly those from Parts I and II. Both oral and written types of exercises are provided, with directions for most exercises clarified by illustrative examples. This material can be worked on during class, with or without reference to Parts I and II, or assigned as homework. It is suggested that the written exercises also be profitably used as oral drills, particularly in the classroom where defects in pronunciation can be corrected by the teacher.

Exercise 1

In each of the following sentences there are two related homophones placed inside the parentheses. Recopy each sentence but omit the homophone that is incorrect.

Example:—Tonight is the last time that that movie will be (shone, shown).
Recopied:—Tonight is the last time that that movie will be shown.

1. Susan has a new fur (wrap, rap).
2. Severe stomach pains and nausea made the patient (wretch, retch).
3. Have you been away. We've (missed, mist) you.
4. The (pore, poor) are always with us.
5. That song is in a (minor, miner) key.
6. That doctor has a roomful of (patience, patients) every day.
7. Will the judge (heed, he'd) the prisoner's (please, pleas) for mercy?
8. Which (one, won) of the boys (one, won) the race?
9. Why isn't the (mail, male) delivered on time?
10. John (guest, guessed) your age correctly, didn't he?

Exercise 2

Write ten original sentences illustrating the correct use of the homophones that you rejected in Exercise 1.

Exercise 3

For each of the blank spaces below find the proper homophone from the two or three related ones indicated in parentheses at the end of each sentence. Then recopy the completed sentences.

Example:—After I walk down the _____ with my bride, _____ take her to some magic _____. (isle, I'll, aisle). Recopied:—After I walk down the aisle with my bride, I'll take her to some magic isle.

1. _____were several people_____who said that they were going to vote for_____favorite candidate. (there, their)
2. Although Al has a sore_____which won't_____, _____walk up the hill with us. (he'll, heal, heel)

3. In the sentence "It is a nice day" _____ _____that the sentence has for_____subject. (it, its, it's)
4. A small boy_____a ball_____our window and broke it. (threw, through)
5. For ten_____you can buy a small bottle of one of those fragrant _____and thrill your_____of smell. (sense, cents, scents)
6. Considering the light_____we were wearing, it was so cold in that room that we had to_____the window. (close, clothes)
7. _____, wearing a sweater of greenish_____, began to_____ down a tree. (hue, Hugh, hew)
8. If John_____that notice of a chance to sail the seven_____, he will_____the opportunity. (seize, sees, seas)
9. Harry said he_____that_____ _____stayed nearly all night and cost him a pretty_____for liquor. (sum, guest, some, guessed)
10. That ancient manuscript which I cannot_____was written on a substance made from a_____called papyrus. (reed, read)

Exercise 4

Each word (homograph) in heavier (blacker) type **rhymes** with only one of the words placed in parentheses. Pronounce the heavy-type word first, then pronounce each of the words in the parentheses. Then cross out the word in the parentheses that doesn't rhyme with the heavy-type word.

Example:—While fishing, I caught a two-pound **bass.** (gas, lace). The word "gas" rhymes with the homograph "bass,²" meaning "fish" but "lace" doesn't. So cross out "lace" which rhymes with "bass¹" meaning a male singer.

1. At the final curtain the actors took a **bow.** (how, go)
2. It's so **close** in here that I want to open a window. (dose, rose)
3. The clergyman **read** from the Bible. (bead, bred)
4. It's time to **mow** my lawn. (cow, go, to)
5. My watch has run down. I'll have to **wind** it. (lined, tinned)
6. That pipe in the bathroom is made of **lead.** (fed, deed, mead)
7. We spent our vacation in **Nice.** (ice, lease)
8. Shakespeare wrote both **prose** and poetry. (goes, lose)
9. There is very heavy **dew** on the grass this morning. (sew, true)
10. The message was sent in Morse **code.** (rod, road)

Exercise 5

Each homograph in heavier type is correctly printed, but it must also be correctly pronounced. Indicate whether the accent is properly on the first or on the second syllable by crossing out either (1) or (2).

Example:—John went to bed early in order to **conserve** his strength for the final examination the next day. (accent on the (1) (2) syllable). "Conserve" should be accented on the second syllable, so cross out (1).

1. Mary's husband didn't **desert** her. (accent on the (1) (2) syllable)
2. Every day the sanitation truck collects our **refuse.** (accent on the (1) (2) syllable)

3. Because the dying man didn't sign his will, it was **invalid**. (accent on the (1) (2) syllable)
4. No street signs may **project** more than three feet in front of the building. (accent on the (1) (2) syllable)
5. Pretty girls always **entrance** young men. (accent on the (1) (2) syllable)
6. Mary likes to perfume her room with **incense**. (accent on the (1) (2) syllable)
7. **Minute** quantities of copper are found in most drinking water. (accent on the (1) (2) syllable)
8. You need a **permit** before you can start driving a car. (accent on the (1) (2) syllable)
9. The teacher will **record** all absences in his book. (accent on the (1) (2) syllable)
10. Cold causes metal to **contract** (accent on the (1) (2) syllable)

Exercise 6

Find the matching homophone of each word in heavy type and then insert this homophone in the blank space in the same sentence.

Example:—Last night I **read** a book printed in _____ ink. The matching homophone is "red."

1. Even a **grown** man will_____when he has severe pains.
2. I told Mother I_____where she got her **new** dress.
3. After a **pause** the cat lunged at and grabbed a mouse with its two_____.
4. Don't_____over your book in that **poor** light.
5. If those kids **ring** that doorbell again, I'll_____their necks.
6. The first **scene** of that opera was the most interesting I have ever _____.
7. **Wait** for me, I want to see what my_____is while I'm near the scales.
8. The **crews** of those ships are being hired for a world_____.
9. Our_____cook will **finish** her vacation in August.
10. Ella_____her **nose** is too long.

Exercise 7

Follow directions in Exercise 6.

1. The truckmen had to **haul** our piano through the_____to the living-room.
2. Each state **capitol** is located in the_____of that state.
3. The choirmaster asked the soprano to sing the_____with **him**.
4. **Joan's** last name is_____.
5. That new boy-scout does **not** yet know how to tie a_____.

6. See the children_____down the playground **chute.**
7. _____better **weed** the garden if we want any potatoes by fall.
8. **Would** you like to buy a_____stove?
9. You can't **sell** anything to the prisoner in his_____.
10. Francis had a bad case of the **grippe,** but now he is better and has a good_____on himself.

Exercise 8

Follow directions given in Exercise 6

1. The **seller** of that wine had his office in his_____.
2. Riding on a **horse** all day in the cold wind made Ann_____.
3. I **pray** my children never become the_____of loan sharks.
4. If John would **heed** the advice of his more experienced father, _____do better in the business world.
5. There is no sales **tax** on a ten-cent box of_____.
6. George **rued** the day he had been_____to his teacher.
7. **Wayne** Smith's fortunes are on the_____.
8. They'll_____that old building and **raise** up a much higher one.
9. The cashier in that bar and **grill** sits behind a_____.
10. We shouted "_____" to the **four** golfers just ahead of us.

Exercise 9

For one of the two homophones in each of the parentheses there is an equivalent (synonym) or definition listed below (a—t). Find this equivalent and write a sentence definition of the homophone followed by the letter of the equivalent.

Example:—Sentence 1. An ant is an insect. (n)

1. (ant, aunt). 2. (bough, bow). 3. (to cede, seed). 4. (dear, deer). 5. (ewe, you). 6. (feign, fane). 7. (file, phial). 8. (him, hymn). 9. (leak, leek). 10. (main, mane). 11. (to mince, mints). 12. (role, roll). 13. (serf, surf). 14. (surge, serge). 15. (strait, straight). 16. (tide, tied). 17. (ton, tun). 18. (waist, waste). 19. (weak, week). 20. (yew, you).

a. a narrow passage by water b. feeble c. rise and fall of the sea d. a Russian peasant e. to chop very fine f. a kind of cloth g. a small bottle h. the actor's part i. a shrine j. a female sheep k. to grant l. arm of a tree m. hair on a horse's neck n. an insect o. a very large container p. a type of evergreen tree q. the center of the human body r. a small onion s. expensive t. a sacred song

Exercise 10

Write twenty original sentences illustrating the correct use of the homophones that you rejected in Exercise 9.

Exercise 11

If any of these pairs of words do not **rhyme,** cross them out.

Example:—Pair no. 7 does not rhyme and should be crossed out. Pair no. 12 does rhyme.

1. Feint—paint. 2. bole—whole. 3. bread—said. 4. heed—head. 5. tie—try. 6. made—lad. 7. seat—sit. 8. his—this. 9. bone—done. 10. thumb—some. 11. great—heat. 12 steal—heal. 13. brews—loose. 14. two—few. 15. tulle—dull. 16. lose—fuse. 17. buy—cry. 18 weight—gate. 19. pear—fear. 20. suit—soot.

Exercise 12

For each homophone in heavy type choose a synonym or word closely equivalent in meaning from the list of words (a—k) below the sentences. Write each synonym within the parentheses following its sentence.

Example:—The word "color" (h) should be written within the parentheses after Sentence 8 because "hue" means "color."

1. That woman is an **anti**-vivisectionist. (   )
2. We had an upper **berth** on the train. (   )
3. We tried to **coax** Father to lend us the car. (   )
4. We had to **dun** our neighbor for the sofa we had sold him. (   )
5. We took a **cruise** to Bermuda. (   )
6. A **stake** marked the boundary between ours and the neighbor's land.
7. The sheep like to **graze** in that field. (   )
8. Her eyes are of violet **hue.** (color)
9. After I had just **lain** down for a nap, the telephone rang. (   )
10. The robbers got away with much rich **loot.** (   )
11. Mary had an **oral** exam in art. (   )

a. feed. b. persuade. c. recline. d. against. e. trip. f. bed. g. post. h. color. i. collect from. j. booty. k. spoken.

Exercise 13

Write ten original sentences illustrating the correct use of the homophones that match or are the counterparts of those in heavy type in Exercise 12.

Example:—Sentence 1. Mother's sister is my auntie. (homophone of **anti**)

Exercise 14

Follow the directions given in Exercise 12.

1. There was a dangerous **fissure** in the ice on the skating pond. (   )
2. Will you **peel** me a peach? (   )
3. They are going to **raze** the building next door. (   )
4. That actress plays the **role** of Lady Macbeth. (   )
5. Some water pipes are made of **lead.** (   )
6. I went to the party and John did **too.** (   )

7. A **maid** took our coats. (   )
8. We yelled "**fore**" to the sluggish golfers ahead of us. (   )
9. There were only some dull coals in the **grate**. (   )
10. Did John **beat** you at chess? (   )

a. part. b. win from. c. tear down. d. remove the skin. e. also. f. a heavy metal. g. look out. h. servant. i. crack. j. part of a stove.

Exercise 15

Write ten original sentences illustrating the use of the homophones that match or are the counterparts of those in heavy type in Exercise 14.

> Example:—Sentence 1. Christ called himself a **fisher** of men. (homophone of **fissure**)

Exercise 16. Oral Drill

Read the following sentences **aloud,** paying particular attention to the correct pronunciation of the homographs in heavy type. Note that the homographs in this exercise vary in **vowel** sound. Check your pronunciation with your teacher or refer to the rhyme key for each homograph listed in Part II, Dictionary of Homographs, on pp. 55–62.

> Example:—"Wind" in Sentence 3 should rhyme with **dined** and **mind.**

1. Don't **hinder** Herb; he has to mow the lawn.
2. I told the minister **we'd wed** on New Year's Day.
3. When I tried to **wind** my watch, I **wound** it too tightly.
4. John had a **row** with his wife after she had gotten water from her **shower** all over the floor.
5. As was my **wont,** I went to **Nice** for the winter.
6. When we buy that farm **we'll** dig a **well, won't** we?
7. John's excuse for not **tarrying** was that he had to go home and **polish** his car.
8. The Sanitation trucks will gather up the garbage in those **rows** of cans.
9. Recently I read the Book of **Job.**
10. I still have the **primer** I used when I began the study of German.

Exercise 17

Write ten original sentences illustrating the correct use of those homographs opposite in **sound** to their counterparts in Exercise 16.

> Example:—Sentence 9. Sam likes to read on the **job.** (rhymes with rob)

Exercise 18. Oral Drill

Follow the directions given in Exercise 16. Note that the homographs in this exercise vary in **accent.**

> Example:—When you pull on a rubber band, it expands; when you release it, it **contracts.** The term **contracts** is accented on the second syllable.

1. I don't like my son to **consort** with undesirable young men.
2. Aspirin brought me **blessed** relief from my headache.
3. She likes to take long walks and **commune** with nature.
4. Because he hadn't signed it, the dead man's will was **invalid.**
5. Have you heard of the **project** to remove rent controls?
6. Don't **incense** your teacher by refusing to do any homework.
7. When wool shrinks, it **contracts.**
8. We are very fond of grape **conserve** with our toast.
9. In the courtroom the witness had to **subject** himself to many hostile questions from the opposing counsel.
10. They served a **buffet** lunch at the club.

Exercise 19

Write ten original sentences illustrating the correct use of the homographs **accented** differently from their counterparts in Exercise 18.

> Example:—Sentence 5. Awnings **project** from my windows. The term **project**² is accented on the **second** syllable.

Exercise 20. Oral Drill

Follow the directions given in Exercise 16. Note that in the following sentences there are both homographs that vary in **vowel sound** and also homographs that vary in **accent.**

1. We sat in the second **tier** of the theatre and watched the magician **conjure** a rabbit out of his hat.
2. Fortunately the family were not **present** when the high **wind** blew down their house.
3. I won't **permit** you to touch that **live** wire. You want to **live,** don't you?
4. If she should **refuse** to cooperate with the nurse, that bedridden **invalid** would **incense** the **intern.**
5. An **aged** priest of **august** appearance read the **collect** in a deep bass voice and **blessed** the sacramental wine.
6. Our electric organ has a **compact console.**
7. Did you have any of that delicious **pâté** that we served at the **buffet?**
8. That **record** store will **record** your voice on a tape.
9. That bus driver gave me a **transfer** which I can **use** on a crosstown bus.
10. You cannot **sow** grain or other seeds in the **desert** and have them grow.

Exercise 21

Write ten original sentences illustrating the correct use of the homographs that differ in sound or accent from their counterparts used in Exercise 20.

Exercise 22

The following sentences made up of misused homophones can make sense if read orally. Read each of these sentences aloud and listen to your voice until you understand the ideas expressed. Then rewrite each sentence with the correct spellings.

> Example:—Martha has blew eyes and a tiny waste. Rewritten:—Martha has blue eyes and a tiny waist.

1. Aisle sea if eye can meat u their.
2. Heal have two bee they're bi too o'clock.
3. Did u mien too bi the hoarse this weak?
4. Cook took sum flower and maid sum do.
5. Heed better he'd his doctor's advice.
6. They awl came accept Mary.
7. Frances says his name sounds just like Francis.
8. Susan is in a very bad mooed because she didn't get enough presence for Christmas.
9. The king sat on his thrown and through a rose to his favorite.
10. At the hospital the patience paste up and down the corridor looking very pail.

Exercise 23

Write ten original sentences illustrating the correct use of the homophones that you rejected in Exercise 22.

Exercise 24

Which homophones in heavy type are used correctly and which ones are used incorrectly? Before you decide check each of them against the list of matching homophones (a—ll) placed below the sentences. Then, making all necessary corrections, recast each sentence.

1. **Hairy's hoarse** has to **hall** a **lode** of hay to the farm.
2. Our teacher is very strict, **sew** you **guise** better know your **lessons.**
3. The **too** enemies fought a **dual** in front of **there** tents.
4. Frank was **borne** in Mexico near the U.S. **border.**
5. **Kernel Joans** is the **idol** of his soldiers.
6. **Weave no knew** friends.
7. She wears **faults hare** and an old **fir** coat.
8. I saw a **whole heard** of sheep **inveighed** the vegetable garden and they **eight awl** the **beet** tops.
9. We **peaked threw** the window **pain** and saw the priest praying at an **altar.**
10. Our **guessed** let out a **grown** when he upset a **bowl** of gravy.

a. all. b. alter. c. ate. d. beat. e. boarder. f. bole. g. born. h. colonel. i. cote. j. duel. k. false. l. fur. m. groan. n. guest. o. guys. p. hair. q. Harry's. r. haul. s. herd. t. hey. u. hole. v. horse. w. idle. x. invade. y. Jones. z. know. aa. lessens. bb. load. cc. new. dd. no. ee. pane. ff. peeked. gg. so. hh. tense. ii. their. jj. through. kk. two. ll. we've.

Exercise 25

Write ten or more original sentences illustrating the correct use of the homophones that you rejected in Exercise 24.

Exercise 26

Each homophone below is followed by two terms one of which is related in meaning or in logical connection to the homophone. Cross out the incorrect term after each homophone.

> Example:—tier—drop of water, row. Cross out drop of water which is a synonym of tear.[1]

1. Knead—find necessary, squeeze
2. reck—break, heed
3. berth—bed, baby
4. grip—sickness, grasp
5. graze—paint, cow
6. currant—berry, electricity
7. coupe—chicken house, car
8. beat—win, vegetable
9. rest—snatch, relax
10. pale—vessel, white
11. plum—fruit, dig
12. sale—bargain, ship
13. cent—smell, smallest U.S. coin
14. naval—ship, orange
15. nun—church, no one
16. stationary—fastened, letter paper

Exercise 27

Follow directions in Exercise 26.

1. rye—drink, bitter
2. weigh—diet, path
3. vane—weather, blood
4. hell—punishment, he will
5. idol—worship, lazy
6. leak—gas, onion
7. lyre—music, teller of untruths
8. loan—bank, alone
9. loot—thief, musical instrument
10. medal—bravery, interfere
11. mince—pie, candy
12. pane—glass, hurt
13. parish—priest, die
14. pearl—jeweler, danger
15. plane—fly, simple
16. yew—a person, a plant

Exercise 28

In the sentences below the words in heavy type are misused homophones. Recopy each sentence and substitute the correct homophones.

1. Mary walked **threw** the doorway.
2. The bride's father **lead** her to the **alter**.
3. Martha bought a dress and had it **rapped** by the saleslady.
4. A **leak** is a small green onion.
5. The opposite of war is **piece**.
6. When it is high **tied**, the ocean comes up **hire** on the **beech**.
7. The pleased dog wagged his **tale**.
8. The master **leeds** his dog on a leash.
9. My creditor told me that I **ode** him $50.
10. We **herd** the church bell **wring**.

Exercise 29

Write ten original sentences illustrating the correct use of the misused homophones in Exercise 28.

Exercise 30

Follow the directions given in Exercise 28.

1. Elizabeth II **rains** in Great Britain at present.
2. Joseph **rode** on the Harvard crew.
3. Several glasses of **bier** were ordered by the group at the large table.
4. The bride received many **presence**.
5. We were astonished to see how much our young nephew had **groan** during the **passed** year.
6. The **too** sisters left all **there** money to a niece.
7. Someone **paste** up and down in front of our house last night.
8. This chicken lacks all **saver**.
9. Harry **war** his **tucks** at the formal dance.
10. The audience was rather **board** with the comedian's stale jokes.

Exercise 31

Write ten original sentences illustrating the correct use of the misused homophones in Exercise 30.

Exercise 32

Recopy each of the following sentences after you have eliminated the misused homophone within the parentheses in each sentence.

1. That (we, wee) lad is only three.
2. Othello was a (Moor, More).
3. We had (mints, mince) pie for dessert.
4. A (pete, peat) fire gives out good heat.

5. You must remember to (baste, based) a roast turkey.
6. How did you (fare, fair) with the car that you borrowed from Jack?
7. That old man walks with an unsteady (gait, gate).
8. We keep our old magazines in the (seller, cellar).
9. Marie wore a diamond (broach, brooch) on her breast.
10. A speeding car hurtled (passed, past) us.

Exercise 33

Write ten sentences illustrating the correct use of the homophones that you rejected in Exercise 32.

Exercise 34

The following letter is full of misused homophones that can make sense if read **orally**. Read this letter aloud slowly, and listen to your voice until you understand the ideas expressed. Then rewrite the letter with all the words correctly spelled.

Example:—Eye haven't herd from u in weaks. Rewritten:—I haven't heard from you in weeks.

Dear Marry:—

Its been daze since wee flue to Bermuda far above the see in a flight so gentle that the plain seamed almost to bee stationery. And how thrilling it was when hour pilate sword above the clouds into the brilliant setting son!

Remember how we used to peddle hour bikes along the shore and then up along the creak to the in where wee staid that to weaks? And those walks down the ruff rode and those turns into the shady lain full of flours. How often I have mist those five o'clock tease as well as those marvelous stakes wee used two broil outdoors their. What fun it was to watch the tied ebb and floe and the waves brake upon the beech. Truly the presents of a friend ads sew much, such a philip, too a Bermudian trip. What a cite those close were that wee wood ware—those gay—knot to say loud—patterned shirts and cocky shorts. Back north in New York its fir cote thyme, and u wood knead two dress much moor warmly. Speaking of fir cotes, I had a peak at sum in Saks last knight.

What a tail eye had too tell when eye got back home and Be and eye poured over the culler prince eye had taken and which eye have never shone u. Pleas rite and tell mi when wee will meat again. Wee simply mussed get together sum dey soon and plan a knew trip.

Affectionately,

LC

Exercise 35

Note:—The homophones used in this exercise are to be found in the supplementary list, Part III, pp. 63–69.

Recopy each sentence but omit the homophone in each parenthesis that is misused. Check the definitions in your dictionary first.

1. A man who catches birds is called a (fouler, fowler).
2. That grocery bag is made of (kraft, craft) paper.
3. Moonshiners make (illicit, elicit) liquor.
4. That's a nice dog you have there, (Sunny, Sonny).
5. The voters felt that Kennedy was Presidential (timber, timbre).
6. A (conk, conch) is a kind of shell.
7. There were hundreds of (sacks, sacs) of Christmas mail in the general postoffice.
8. Today most railroads have standard (gage, gauge) track.
9. That mentally disturbed person is going to his (annalist, analyst).
10. By the looks of those dark clouds a thunderstorm is (imminent, immanent).

Exercise 36

Write ten original sentences illustrating the correct use of the homophones that you rejected in Exercise 35.

Exercise 37

Follow directions given in Exercise 35.

1. No (better, bettor) always wins his wagers.
2. Tim likes to lie on a bench and (laze, lays).
3. The Army bugle (core, corps) played in the parade.
4. We use a glass pyrex (pi, pie) plate when baking a pie.
5. I've (all ready, already) spent all of my weekly allowance.
6. At the meeting my motion was carried without any (dissent, descent).
7. John was (peaked, piqued, peeked) because he didn't get the (raise, raze) that he had been promised.
8. The auto dealer has a (lien, lean) on that car he sold Brown.
9. I'll carry two of the packages and you carry the (wrest, rest).
10. We drove through Central Park in a (handsome, hansom) cab.

Exercise 38

Write ten original sentences illustrating the use of the homophones that you rejected in Exercise 37.

Exercise 39

Follow directions given in Exercise 35.

1. People like to (brute, bruit) about rumors of disaster.
2. That new baby is a welcome (edition, addition) to that small family.

3. Their father was strict and his children always (towed, toed) the mark.
4. Mrs. Williams will (oversea, oversee) the children at the birthday party.
5. The priest read to his congregation from his (missal, missile).
6. Arthur doesn't look well in shorts because his knees are (nobby, knobby).
7. That policeman carried a large (pistil, pistol).
8. The kids on the street were making such a (racket, racquet) that I had to (clothes, close) the windows.
9. We watched for the sputnik, but it never came (in sight, incite).
10. Ted was injured in football during his (adolescence, adolescents).

Exercise 40

Write ten original sentences illustrating the use of the homophones that you rejected in Exercise 39.